The Masters Path

How to Intentionally Create More Happiness, Joy and Fulfillment in Your Life

J. John St. James

Copyright © 2022 by John St. James

All rights reserved.

No part of this publication may be reproduced, distributed, or transmitted in any form or by any means, including photocopying, recording, or other electronic or mechanical methods, without the prior written permission of the author, except in the case of brief quotations embodied in critical reviews and certain other noncommercial uses permitted by copyright law.

Visit the Official Website at:
Printed in the United States of America

First Printing: June 2022

John St. James

ISBN-13: 979-8-218-01010-2

John St. James books may be purchased for educational, business or sales promotional use. Special discounts are available on quantity purchases.

For orders by U.S. trade bookstores and wholesalers,
please contact John St. James via telephone at (770) 547-2511
or via email at stjames.jsj@gmail.com.

Disclaimer

While the Author and Publisher have strived to be as accurate and complete as possible in the creation of this book, readers are cautioned to rely on their own judgment about their individual circumstances to act accordingly.

While all attempts have been made to verify information provided in this publication, the author and publisher assumes no responsibility for errors, omissions, or contrary interpretation of the subject matter herein. Any perceived slights of specific persons, peoples, or organizations are unintentional. This book details the author's own personal experiences and opinions.

The author and publisher are providing this information on an "as is" basis and make no representations or warranties of any kind with respect to this book or its contents. The author and publisher disclaim all such representations and warranties including, for example, warranties of merchantability and educational advice for a particular purpose. In addition, the author and publisher do not represent or warrant that the information accessible via this book is accurate, complete or current.

Except as specifically stated in this book, neither the author or publisher, nor any authors, contributors, or other representatives will be liable for damages arising out of, or in connection with, the use of the content in this book. This is a comprehensive limitation of liability that applies to all damages of any kind, including (without limitation) compensatory; direct, indirect or direct, indirect or consequential damages; loss of data, income or profit; loss of or damage to property and claims of third parties.

You understand that this book is not intended as a substitute for consultation with a licensed professional. In the event you use any of the information in this book for yourself, which is your constitutional right, the author and publisher assume no responsibility for your actions or outcomes.

Dedication

To my wife Mercy

To my father and mother
who taught me the "hero's" mindset

To my students, clients, and friends;
I am grateful for all your support

Acknowledgments

I don't know where to start. So many terrific people helped me and supported me in this project.

To my mentors: Grandmaster Stephen Washington, Dr. John C. Maxwell, and Darren Hardy, who taught me how to live a life of significance.

My incredible friends: Glenn Adams, cousins Linda Major, and Alison Masick, who helped me with a first read edit. My students, especially Master Paul Harmon, who helped with formatting, Travis Cody (Inspired Solutions) helped with marketing, and Angie Droulias, who helped with developmental and copy-editing.

A special thanks to Mr. Paul Lopez at 1220 Media for all his help with graphics and additional formatting suggestions.

To all of you who inspired me to write this book, you have been true heroes along the Master's Path.

Table of Contents

Dedication iii
Acknowledgments iv
Introduction.. 1

PHASE 1 Learning and Growing................................ **11**
Chapter 1 Getting Started Mindfully 13
Chapter 2 Living Intentionally.................................... 31
Chapter 3 Acting Courageously with Confidence.... 41

PHASE 2 Sharing and Serving................................... **53**
Chapter 4 Making a Major Positive Impact 55
Chapter 5 Learn, Grow, Share, Serve, Lead, and Inspire 67
Chapter 6 Leadership Core Competencies 87
Chapter 7 Mastering Strategic Planning and
　　　　　 Warrior Tactics................................... 107
Chapter 8 Mastering the Circle of Responsibility....131

PHASE 3 Leading and Inspiring............................... **143**
Chapter 9 Living an Empowering Life While Being
　　　　　 a Catalyst for Positive Change.............. 145
Chapter 10 The Power to Raise People Up 155

Chapter 11 Living Honorably 167
Chapter 12 Taking the Challenge... 177
Chapter 13 The Power of Perserverance 195
Chapter 14 The X Factor of Success: Growth Mindset
              with the Discipline of the Master 209
Chapter 15 The Discipline of the Master............................... 225
Chapter 16 The Spiritual Gift of the Artist 233
About the Author... 251

Introduction

Dear Hero,

I would first like to congratulate you on taking your first step towards attaining mastery, which begins with purchasing this book. You may not realize it at this point, but you are in for a life-altering experience – one that is backed up by years of research, tried and tested programs, and transformative results.

Allow me to introduce myself. My name is John St. James and I am an internationally certified life coach and an 8th-degree black belt in traditional martial arts. I also run an international martial arts organization and the World Leadership Foundation. I have been coaching successful people like you for over 45 years. Within those years I have started several successful businesses, coached world champions, and have clients ranging from medical doctors, attorneys, and entrepreneurs to moms and dads who are looking to take their lives to the next level and beyond. In short, I work with successful people to provide positive, lasting transformation.

The Master's Path is based on my **Transformation to Total Practitioner (T3P) Elite Coaching Program**. A program that equips the learner – the leader, CEO, entrepreneur, instructor, coach, or team lead – with the necessary mental, emotional and spiritual tools to **attract what they want in life** and **magnetize success** through strategic exercises and consistent habits.

The result: Nothing short of **true transformation**. And it all begins with your mindset and mental habits.

There is scientific proof that your mind is capable of miracles. As you develop your potential, you will experience the extraordinary. You will become a super-achiever. Imagine improving every aspect of your life. It is not only possible; it's probable with time and commitment.

Why You're Here and What to Expect

I addressed you as "Hero" because within you, and within each of us, lies a massive amount of potential — it is that same potential that has brought you here.

Success experts say human beings only use 5 to 15 percent of that natural potential. That means we have as much as 85% more potential within ourselves to manifest the life and financial security that we want. As a professional coach for the last 45 years, I can personally share how to utilize that **85% potential**.

Just ask yourself the question: "What do I want to manifest in my life right now?"

We all have dreams and the desire to live the good life. To succeed. To learn. To excel in all that we do. But here's the problem: how do we do that?

Remember when you were a kid and dreamed about a time when you would be in charge of your destiny, and nothing could stop you from being what you wanted to be? As an adult, you

Introduction

have the authority you wished for as a child, but things aren't going as planned.

It's your life, and you deserve life's very best. So do your family, friends, and the community at large. But, admittedly, most people in the world today aren't feeling that great right now. Maybe you yourself are feeling…

… like life is all work and no play.

… uneasy about your future.

… anxious about your financial security.

… that you want to give up on your hopes and dreams because they are not being realized.

… a lack of the gratification that you had hoped to have achieved years ago.

… a sense of being "stuck" in the same place for too long.

… a hole, gap, or the sense of something missing from life.

Via the theory and practical exercises outlined in this book, I will show you how you can **take your life to the next level and beyond.** Because – and this might come as a shock – sheer potential is not enough. Most people talk about what they want, but only a small number of people take action to make their dreams become a reality. The truth of life is that you will not achieve what you want in life if you don't take action.

But how do you even get started? Well, it all starts with a **mentor or guide.** You need a mentor or a coach to accelerate your progress by providing focus and awareness of how to use your life energy.

This book gives you access to the curriculum from my T3P Elite Coaching Program; essentially, you already have a coach to guide you through those very first steps to mastery. Additional mentorship can be sought during or after, but only if you wish to.

I will be sharing wisdom from many of the most successful people I have studied over the last 40 years to give you new perspectives and resources to make your life easier and more fun.

As your guide or mentor, it's my sacred mission to assist you in producing extraordinary results in your life and as an entrepreneur. Our goal is to be happy, healthy, loved, and supported throughout the journey, not just for a destination of money or wealth.

Using the **proven techniques** in this book, you can expect to:

- Do some life-changing introspection
- Improve your professional performance
- Enhance the quality of your personal life
- Overcome fears and doubts that keep you in a loop of low self-esteem and limitation
- Break free from soulless routines and bad habits
- Get in touch with your passions, dreams, and true purpose
- Find your own solutions, even during the hardest of times
- Boost your motivation and willpower
- Improve the relationship with yourself and with others
- Build a solid foundation so that your greatest potential for learning, achievement, and success can be utilized

Introduction

- Leverage success by taking our "Intellectual Capital" and multiplying it
- Identify where you want to go in the future and your desired outcome
- Learn to control your negative internal reactions
- Learn how to create intentions, choices, and actions that will help activate the remaining 85% of natural talent and potential within you that is just waiting to be tapped
- Reclaim your childhood dream of an empowered life
- Design your best life ever!

Do any of these sound like something you would like to achieve? If so, keep reading!

How to Use This Book

You have now gauged that *The Master's Path* is a transformational coaching program distilled into a single book. But that doesn't mean that you should be casual about it and, ultimately, about your journey. A book is not an excuse to slack or take the journey lightly.

The journey covers three phases:

- **The Master's Path** – We define a master as someone who lives a life of excellent service. The path is your life's journey.
- **The Hero** – We define as an ordinary person who does extraordinary things in extraordinary times.
- **Becoming A Warrior or Champion**– We define a warrior or champion as a peak performer in mind, body, and spirit who strives to be their best daily.

Here are my tips on how to use the book:

Step 1: Claim Responsibility

Wise teachers have said that the day you take complete responsibility for yourself, the day you stop making excuses, is when you start to the top. The day you stop blaming others for your shortcomings is the day you begin the ascent.

Your power of choice is your one true personal power, and it is your greatest ally as you design your destiny. As a mentor and professional success coach, I believe that **our decisions**, not the conditions of our lives, determine our future and destiny.

You must realize that you are responsible for fulfilling all your dreams. The power to succeed or fail is always yours to choose. Today, choose to be a student of success principles and be a lifetime learner. No one can take knowledge away from you. And only you can take action. Wisdom paired with the power of action is the true secret to wealth in life as an entrepreneur, leader, instructor, coach, or team lead. All top executives and athletes use coaches; so, why not you?

But only about 10% of the people who receive life-changing information will put it to use. Everyone starts but less than 10% finish, and even fewer finish well. It takes **desire, commitment, and consistency** to fulfill your fullest potential.

Step 2: Seek out a Mentor (but only if you want to)

You may contact me at my email address and know it will be my pleasure to help you to the next level and beyond. Please refer to my website for information on finding a coach to mentor you: www.johnstjames.com

Introduction

Step 3: Grab a Journal

The journey is peppered with action steps and practical challenges. For this purpose and more, I strongly recommend you **have a journal within reach** as you explore each chapter. Keeping a journal will not only facilitate your learning experience but will also help you move more quickly towards your goals and have a clearer vision of what those goals are.

I strongly recommend you journalize, not just your victories, but also your defeats. Consider *The Master's Path* a game. It is the game of life. Have fun and enjoy the path as you make the ascent. Go at your own pace but do accept **The Call to Greatness**.

Find a success partner or accountability buddy to get the most out of the journey. I call this **Transformation to Total Practitioner** or "T3P" for short. I am happy to serve as your mentor if you want one or don't already have one to serve in this vital role. Either way, know you are not alone on the path.

Step 4: Apply the Power of Three

To get the most out of our journey, you will need to use the Power of Three, which is:

1. Application
2. Accountability
3. Acceptance

Remember, it's not more information but rather more **application**. Knowledge is only potential power. It is the application of knowledge or taking action where the rubber meets the road.

Accountability will help you stay on track. It will also help you make quick adjustments when they are needed most. Working with an advisor or mentor that has walked the path before you will help you avoid drift.

Acceptance will help ground you. We are all exactly where we are supposed to be at this time in our journey. If you are not where you want to be, it starts with acceptance and commitment to change. The Master's Path is an excellent starting point to help you learn, grow, share, serve, lead, and inspire. Accepting "The Call" and taking responsibility for your life leads to tremendous success.

Step 5: Complete Each Exercise and Challenge – NO Excuses!

Each exercise (known as the **Quest Challenge**) is mandatory along your journey.

As you proceed from one exercise to another, you will pile one success on top of another. With time, energy, and patience, you will strengthen your confidence, knowledge, attitude, skills, and habits. As your journey progresses, you will begin to achieve extraordinary accomplishments — things you may have long considered impossible and unattainable.

You can even score yourself on **"To Be"** and **"Not to Be"** behaviors related to transformative tenets, code, and attitudinal requirements. Below is an example of one possible **T3P "To Be"** list to include the following considerations:

Introduction

<u>To Be = Moving Towards</u>

- To be more thoughtful and or mindful
- To be more intentional
- To serve and or volunteer more
- To be more positive
- To be more courageous
- To be the example more often
- To lead more
- To have a servant mentality more often
- To be a team player, more
- To be honorable more often
- To be committed more
- To be growing and improving your knowledge, attitude, skills, and habits more
- To inspire more often
- To be more creative
- To be more caring and compassionate
- To persevere more in the face of adversity
- To be a person of good character
- To be more loving
- To be more adventurous
- To be more encouraging and supportive
- To be more proactive
- To be more professional
- To be more humble
- To make a significant impact more often

Not To Be = Moving Away From

You create your list as only you know what areas you need to strengthen. If you need help with this, I suggest you speak with your advisor or mentor. You might also talk with your spouse or significant other.

There is never a better time to become all you can be. The Master's Path is your opportunity to seize life. It is your opportunity to take it to a whole new level.

I welcome you on the path, Hero.

> *"We can't change our circumstances until we change ourselves." – Jim Rohn*

PHASE 1
Learning and Growing

Chapter 1

Getting Started Mindfully

"The journey of a thousand miles begins with one step." – Lao Tzu

Welcome to the very first chapter, and your first mindful step on the hero's journey. Chapter 1 is all about setting the preliminary foundations for what you will come to learn and master as you navigate the book. We will focus on asking the right questions and getting your 'mental toolkit' together so you can get from where you are to where you want to be. You will also learn to motivate others while challenging yourself.

If you apply all the tactics and techniques in this chapter and this book, you will begin to achieve extraordinary results in everything you do.

Start Here: The 10 Ingredients for Full Potential Mastery

Extraordinary results aren't viable unless you are fully equipped with the right tools to get you there – that is, ultimately, to your fullest potential. If you already have a mentor, the path will be made easier. If you don't, you can use this book as your guide.

Here are the **ten ingredients** you will need to get started if you aim to master your manifestation skills and create the best life possible thanks to your fullest potential:

1. **Desire** – You must have a burning passion. It must be an all-consuming obsession. You must fall in love with personal growth and development, which includes a big enough why.

    Ask yourself: What are you passionate about? What do you wholeheartedly enjoy doing? What lifts you out of a bad mood if you do it? What would you do even if nobody paid you for it or noticed you?

2. **Belief** – Challenge your old ideas and limiting beliefs about yourself and your life in general. Listen to those who believe in you and borrow their faith if you have to.

    Ask yourself: What idea or belief about yourself have you been fostering for too long? Has it served you in any way or are you simply holding onto it due to habit? How do your friends and peers react to this belief? Do they counter this idea with their own beliefs? And can their beliefs help you change?

3. **Action** – The Master's Path is, first and foremost, an action philosophy.

Getting Started Mindfully

Ask yourself: Is there an opportunity in your life that you can currently seize? What is holding you back from taking action? Imagine you have removed whatever is holding you back – would you take action then?

4. **Courage** – Take the first step without knowing any of the others. Be willing to be afraid, and as the old Nike slogan goes, "Just do it!"

   Ask yourself: What stifles your courage? Is it overthinking? Insecurity? Fear? What are the ingredients you need to create a courageous life and attitude?

5. **The Power of Yes** - You must find your "Yes". Be in relentless pursuit of your dream, no matter what.

   Ask yourself: What makes you say "YES"? What pricks up your ears when you hear about it or makes your heart thump when you are about to do it?

6. **Don't Negotiate** – Don't negotiate with your dream. Be willing to pay the price no matter what.

   Ask yourself: What do you want to achieve more than anything? Does the price matter? Do the sacrifices matter? Does the effort matter? If they do, then you don't want your dream passionately enough.

7. **Creativity** – Be creative. Focus on possibilities, not limitations.

   Ask yourself: What brings out your creative juices? What creative activity could you lose yourself in for hours on end? Can the creative skills you make use of in that practice be transferred to other parts of your life?

8. **Sacrifice** – Let go of good and make room for better. Move from good to better and better to best.

Ask yourself: What good in your current circumstance can become better? What can be improved? Could you be limiting yourself by claiming that only certain things can be improved while other things can't? And what bad or mediocre thing can you completely let go of?

9. **Vision** – See yourself in possession of what you desire. Hold your image and do it with feeling and frequency.

   Ask yourself: What do you want more than ever? Can you envision it happening daily?

10. **Celebrate** – Celebrate victories along the way and learn from failures. Take time to recognize success, and it will surely come. Remember, your perspective determines your potential.

    Ask yourself: What good things in your life aren't you celebrating or taking for granted? Can you start celebrating as of now? If so, how would you do this?

Having the Right Mindset and Attitude Along the Path

Now that you know the ten ingredients you need to achieve your fullest potential, should you rustle them up into a super-power cocktail and gulp it down, expecting miraculous results? Well, no, because it doesn't work that way. You can, of course, start cultivating each daily, but you also need to work on yourself and your attitude before embarking on the path.

Here are some **mindset and attitude tips** to get you started:

1. **Find your leverage or hinge points.** These include your most essential functions, projects, and priorities. Take time

to allocate enough time, attention, and life-force capacity or energy (resources) to them.

2. **Find that one priority or project every day and give your whole heart and devotion to it.** Work on it first before you get distracted with everything else that will come your way.

3. **Create "SMART" goals** (**S**pecific, **M**easurable, **A**ttainable, **R**elevant, and **T**ime-bound.) Be sure to use timeframes that challenge you. Remember, it is not more time but more intensity.

4. **Forget normal**. Focus on the extraordinary. Expect great things to happen and expect positive change. The status quo is often not good enough. Remember, the one thing in life that is constant is change. It is up to you whether it is positive or negative.

5. **Make your life worth living.** Manufacture luck by deciding in advance what you want and then making it happen.

6. **Live like a lion.** Don't sweat the small stuff unless you need to. Focus on the big stuff as much as possible. Lead with courage and yet take the time to eat right and sleep as you need it.

7. **Pay attention to the details.** The devil lies in the details, as the old saying goes. Remember, the little things don't mean a little; they mean a lot.

8. **Get rid of the negative.** Focus on the positive. Make it your mantra and repeat, "I don't do negative." Remember, your perspective determines your potential.

9. **Plan for the worst and expect the best.** There will be downturns, pandemics, illnesses, and other unexpected

misfortunes. Have a disaster or relief plan in place, and be ready when you need it.

10. **Be flexible.** Stay limber in mind, body, and spirit. Think of ways to stretch yourself constantly. Whether in business or personal relationships, you are always best to have an open mind and remain flexible.

11. **Overcome fear.** Get rid of the illusion by doing the very thing that scares you. Do this repeatedly, and overcome the fear and terror barrier.

12. **Start before you are ready.** Learn as you go. As the Nike slogan states: "Just do it." The truth is that very few are ever fully prepared. We can't always choose our time, but we can choose to start.

13. **Find your genius.** What are your strengths? Once you know your wheelhouse, stay in it. You are unique. There is not another person exactly like you. Double down on your unique strengths.

14. **Bring your love to work**. Winners value the process. It is not the destination but rather the journey that truly matters.

15. **Trust your gut.** Intuition speaks to us. We have to learn to listen.

16. **Have no regrets.** Take chances and learn from them. Live more fully as you become the person you were meant to be.

17. **Show more gratitude and pay it forward.** Gratitude is the most magical force, especially when you pay it forward. Be grateful for what you have and what you can become. Be a net positive by helping, healing, and sharing your

spiritual gift of excellent service to others. Whatever help you have been given, please pay it forward.

Lessons to Expect

The road to attracting a successful life is also paved with **lessons** – pit stops where you can take a quick breather, upgrade, and repair before moving on to the next one with your newly acquired gear – your acquired knowledge. The lessons should, like pit stops for pro-car racers, be noted on your map. You should expect them to be there and know how to tackle them, even before embarking on the Journey.

Consider the following **three fundamental lessons** to attracting what you want – and be ready, or at least not surprised, when they arise:

> **Lesson # 1:** Success comes from the compound effect.
> Small steps lead to quantum improvement over time. This is also known as the Law of Incremental Improvement.

> **Lesson # 2:** You can have anything you want in life just as long as you are willing to help enough other people get what they want.
> If you want more success for yourself, the fast way to get it is to go about helping someone else obtain it. Look for ways to provide excellent service.

> **Lesson # 3:** Upside/Down/Inside/Out.
> The journey requires that you study with the best (upside) and convert the lessons into plans (down). Once it has become an indelibly etched success habit (inside), you must put it to practice (outside). This process is truly transformative.

The Quest Challenge Explained

I have found that there are specific vital traits or attributes common to all super-achievers. While we will explore these in detail in the chapters to follow, we will also focus on application by working through exercises to help you along the Master's Path. Working through the activities – known as *Quest Challenges* – will quickly attract what you want most.

Are you ready to get started with the first application? The first Quest Challenge?

Just before we do, I want to recap by going over several critical takeaways. They are:

1. **Focus on desire** first but back it up with application as soon as possible.
2. **Work with a guide** or mentor, as accountability and belief are critical to your success.
3. **Expect good things** to happen. Positive expectancy is essential for total transformation.

It is also essential that you consistently apply:

1. Key concepts
2. Key tactics
3. Key strategies

Lastly, always reflect on the following three statements (using your journal would be ideal here):

1. I am grateful for _____.
2. I need to become _____.
3. I will accomplish _____.

GETTING STARTED MINDFULLY

We are now ready to look more closely at the Quest Challenge. It is a simple construct to help keep you on track as you follow the Master's Path. It will help you avoid drift as you get busy with life. Remember, if life is worth living, it is worth recording. As discussed earlier, you must keep a journal to get the most out of this program.

With the help of each action-driving Quest Challenge, you will pile one success on top of another as you move from one chapter to another. With time, energy, and patience, you will strengthen your confidence and knowledge, attitude, skills, and habits to become the Master of your own Path and attract the life you desire.

At the end of each chapter, you will find a place to record your points, scores, and victories. It is your responsibility to keep your journal up-to-date, purposeful, and well-structured; for example, you can **structure each Quest Challenge entry** like so:

- Date
- Sacred Mission
- Quest Challenge/Segment Focus
- Application Exercises
- Duration/Frequency
- Ideas/Insights
- Reflections

We will cover the details of each specific Quest Challenge as we progress along the Master's Path. Be sure to go through all exercises as you get to them.

Quest Challenge: Taking the First Step

Let's get started with your very first Quest Challenge. Take a couple of minutes and answer the following questions. Do this and you have taken the first step in the hero's journey along the Master's Path.

1. Who am I?
2. What makes me really happy?
3. What would my life be like if nothing got in my way?
4. What skills do I need to become unstoppable?
5. How can I serve at the highest level?

Quest Challenges like this will be peppered throughout the book each time an important concept is taught. Look out for them and don't EVER skip them!

The STAR Formula

Before we move onto the fascinating topic of mindfulness and how to leverage its tools on the Master's Path, I want to share something that I feel is very important to your success. It has to do with giving your best. You can effortlessly achieve this if you implement **the STAR Formula** which all heroes use:

> STOP, THINK, ACT, REVIEW

STOP: Pause before taking any kind of action (this is where mindfulness comes in).

THINK: Think about the action you are either about to do or avoid. Weigh the pros and cons, and see the results clearly

ACT: Take action once clarity is achieved.

REVIEW: Review and revise your victories and losses, without judgment.

THE STAR FORMULA

Another way to translate this formula is as:

| SUCCESS THROUGH ACCEPTING RESPONSIBILITY |

No matter how you view it, the STAR Formula should become your guide for every action you ponder on taking.

Why Be Mindful?

The STAR Formula's STOP step is an exercise in mindfulness. But what is mindfulness? And what does it mean to live mindfully?

Contrary to what most people believe, mindfulness is not about having a "full mind"! Rather it's about emptying the mind, and being **fully immersed in the present moment**.

Mindfulness can help you turn chaos into structure with meaning and purpose. This is a tall order, I know. Especially in the world we live in today.

The truth is that our greatest gift is also our greatest challenge. Free choice is wonderful when one takes the time to think through things thoroughly. This said, without the opportunity of order, we can unconsciously choose chaos, which many people do.

Chaos is nothing more than uncontrolled thinking or, if you prefer, a lack of mindfulness. The opposite of this is structured thinking or being mindful. Curriculum One of this course covers how to start down the path of thinking in a structured way.

The **benefits of mindfulness** are great. Here are just a few:

- You will have less stress
- You will have a feeling of being in control
- You will be thinking on purpose rather than by accident
- You will become more alert, aware, conscious, and clear
- You will learn how to become attentive and more intentional

Now, you may be wondering: *How can I best apply mindfulness along the Master's Path?*

Think of mindfulness as a form of **deep awareness**. The Master's Path *is* a journey of self-discovery, which leads to *more* awareness and, for some, enlightenment. That said, it is not easy. In fact, it will be one of the hardest things you will ever do. The effort, however, will be well worth it when you consider just some of **the uses of being mindful.** Here are just a few:

- Eliminating procrastination
- Setting the right intention
- Discovering your true-life purpose
- Creating a desired outcome effortlessly
- Finding true love and happiness
- Helping others to heal
- Discovering yourself, knowing yourself, and mastering yourself

To reach such lofty goals, the practitioner will take a journey that requires not only knowing but more importantly *doing.*

But the ultimate goal of utilizing mindfulness and self-awareness is this: **to become one with nature.** This refers to the nature both around us and within us; the macrocosm and the microcosm, and ultimately, the **whole-person concept.**

To develop the whole person concept, it is best to understand the universal laws of nature and how they interact with everything we do. Unfortunately, most people miss this important connection. In fact, we often hear how it is human nature to act a certain way. Often times this "way" of acting is in direct contradiction of the natural or universal laws. In other words, the person is out of balance with the laws of nature and as such is unbalanced.

We want to act in a way that brings us closer to our goals rather than farther away from them. To do this we must seek to better understand ourselves through heightened awareness and with mindfulness.

The Law of Awareness: Getting the Most Out of Your Journey

You must know yourself to grow yourself. To grow yourself, you must know…

- Your strengths
- Your weaknesses
- Your interests
- Your opportunities

A pivotal part of the Master's Path program is to train our minds, bodies, and spirits. Our goal is always to strive for mastery using state-of-the-art peak performance training with proven methods and philosophies. This is not new and, in fact, has been the path to mastery for as long as humans have been alive. It is often referred to as the "wisdom traditions".

There are **two simple requirements** to ensure you get the most out of your journey. They are:

1. **Be open to change** or, as one of my teachers once told me, "Empty your cup."
2. **Learn and apply** (live) what you learn from the journey. I call this "closing the gap between knowledge and doing" or "turning intent into action".

It is that simple and that hard.

Quest Challenge: GAP Analysis

We have probably all heard the saying, "The biggest room in the world is the room for improvement." To help insure you make mindfulness a part of your everyday existence, I have included a way to help you pay attention to whether you are living what you have learned (i.e., know) and what you do (take action on). This is called a **GAP analysis**.

To do this successfully you will learn how to become the *observer*. You will also learn about *tracking*, which is simply keeping track of what you are doing.

One of the easiest ways to do this is to make living mindfully a game. Keep score and be exceptional. How you may ask?

Your actions are the only true indication of your intentions and ability. This is why the Master's Path is focused on you taking a leadership role in your own life. Look at your life as the game of life. Give yourself points or rewards for taking positive, proactive, life-changing action, rather than just learning more information. In this case, it's not more information but rather more and better application that counts. You get rewarded for action that leads to more positive results and accomplishments.

To do this, simply...

1. Open to a blank page in your journal.
2. Create a header "Scores and Points".
3. Record your actions that demonstrate mindfulness or structured thinking each day.

4. Give them a score. The larger the impact the larger the score.
5. After pre-determined intervals, reward yourself with something that you love to do.

It's that simple. Here's an example...

5/20/15 – Meditated or prayed for 15 to 20 minutes = + 20 points

In the above example, you scored 20 points. You could then reward yourself when you hit 100, 500, 1,000, 3,000, 5,000 and so forth depending on where you start in the game of life. You determine when your actions deserve a reward.

To better help you, here is a list of things to be mindful of:

- Your health
- Your relationships
- Your happiness
- Your chosen career or livelihood
- Your mindset (positive or negative)
- Your contribution
- Your finances including all other resources
- Your focus
- Your habits
- Your time
- Your energy
- Your weaknesses
- Your goals
- Your service

Getting Started Mindfully

Use this chapter to take stock of where you are and where you want to be. Start at the beginning. Set a goal for each of the major areas of your life. This is called the **Circle of Responsibility**, which we will cover in more detail in a later chapter. It requires planning and, most importantly, awareness and clarity. The Japanese word for this is *Zanshin* or "hyper-alertness".

Understand that, to become the master of your life, you need to take full responsibility for your thoughts, words, choices, actions, and habits. To achieve life mastery and be worthy of a life well-lived, you must take ownership and responsibility for your choices. This requires self-awareness first and foremost. It also requires courage, as you will have to face one of your greatest enemies and overcome them.

What is your greatest enemy, you ask? Only *you* can answer that. For many, it is their ego. The truth is that some people would rather "look good" than make a major difference.

As with all things, what you put in is what you will get out. And as you give, you have more to offer. To give more, you have to become more. If you give yourself entirely to your life's journey, you will, in time, master the Path.

Chapter 2

Living Intentionally

"If you aim at nothing, you will hit it every time." – Zig Ziglar

This chapter will bring you a step closer to living intentionally. It may sound pretty self-explanatory, but a select few people only ever manage to live and enjoy an intention-driven life. The key to unlocking intention is through not only the mindfulness approach but through understanding the ingredients your intention is made of and fueled by.

Energy and Attention

You've probably heard the phrase "Energy flows where attention goes". But how do the two relate? And how can we make the most of it on our journey to life mastery?

Let's start with a simple truth: **energy**, **time** and **resources** are your greatest assets.

The truth is, your life and mine are made of the same ingredients. We exist within the construct of time, energy, and resources and they are closely related. You'll begin to unravel how and why as you explore this book.

Consider your own daily energy usage. What do you spend it on? Does it relate to your time? And what sort of resources do you have? For example, working out at the gym is only possible if you have the time to go there and the equipment (resources) to train.

What keeps these three assets together? You guessed right: Attention!

If you pay attention to your energy levels, you will know when to hit the gym and when to rest. If you pay attention to your time, you will know when to allocate gym days to your busy schedule. And if you pay attention to your resources, be that the gym fee or the equipment required, you can make it all happen.

Does it now make more sense when we state that energy flows depending on where you direct your attention? And there's more to this correlation than just my previous examples. Where you put your attention will either **increase or decrease your energy** and will also affect the **quality or value of your time**. Your time, energy, and resources will either be in balance or out of balance.

Your *intention* and, with it, your *attention*, will and does affect your results, and with it your future happiness.

Heroes Take AIM

The acronym for **AIM** is…

> **ATTENTIVE – INTENTIONAL – MINDFUL**

Without proper AIM, you will be **MIA: "Mi**ssing **I**ntentional **A**ction".

TAKING AIM

Taking AIM sets the right intention and helps to ensure positive action.

I'd like to stress the importance of AIM by presenting a martial arts analogy: In martial arts, we use proper aim to focus our energy on a specific target. Whether it is a wooden board, a padded target, or an opponent's anatomy, the process starts with awareness and attention to detail. The practitioner uses intention to channel their power to a specific point. For example, when striking a heavy bag, the practitioner focuses on where they want to land their strike. It requires being mindful of the distance, timing, speed, and power needed to ensure maximum impact. Most importantly, it takes focus and or concentration to hit the mark.

When we aim correctly, we focus mental and physical power on a specific point. Much like setting thoughtful goals, energy flows where attention goes. If our aim is attentive, intentional, and mindful, your focus will be precise and powerful.

Taking AIM with Your Time

You drastically increase your chances of accomplishing your number one vital task with less effort when you increase the quality of your time through **setting the right intention** and **placing your attention** on your life's major purpose.

Just knowing this can change your journey from one of a wayward traveler to a hero conquering the Master's Path. Setting the right intention often leads to **the compound effect**. That is, your results will grow exponentially over time.

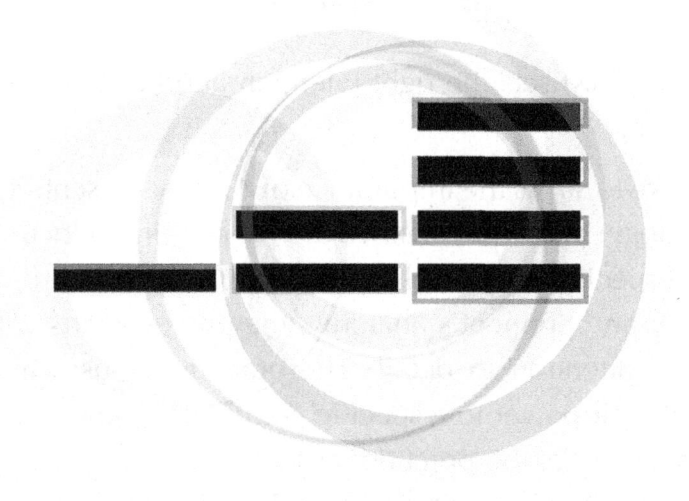

THE COMPOUND EFFECT

Setting the right intention also leads to **the ripple effect**. It will bring to you things that you can only imagine right now – and even some you can't. Like a pebble thrown into a pond, energy travels outwards and attracts like energy.

One of My Earliest Life Examples of Setting the Right Intention

I was competing at the 1969 Junior Olympic Long Course Swimming Championships at Fort Bragg, North Carolina, in the ten and under age group. My specialty was the 200-meter individual medley.

I went into the swim believing I could win my division with a record time for my age group, as I had practiced hard and knew the time I had to beat. I had prepared six days a week for years for the attempt. Most days, I swam in the morning before school under the watchful eye of coach Sawyer for one hour, and then again after school for two hours to develop the skillset and times necessary. I started swimming competitively at the age of five in 1964.

On the day of the meet, I was prepared mentally, physically, and emotionally, and it paid off. I had done the work and had set my intention correctly. I ended up setting a state record for my age group and then went on to set a second state record the same day in the 200-meter freestyle which wasn't my specialty.

I will never forget driving to the meet with my father that day and realizing I didn't have my favorite swimsuit – my lucky charm – with me. My father, seeing how upset I was, turned the car around and rushed back to the hotel where we fetched the swimsuit. On that day, I experienced the power of taking **AIM** by setting the right intention and it led to victory.

The right thoughts are the product of intentionality and proper training. It all starts with a disciplined mind and the gumption or spirit to attempt something that pulls you out of your comfort zone.

Life Is a Trial & Error Proposition – A Different Lesson Along the Path

I remember many years ago doing a demonstration as a 2nd degree black belt where I was attempting to break seven cinder blocks. It was the mid-80s and I was living in Irvine, California. I was in my mid-20s and had no fear, or so I thought.

Prior to the attempt, my thoughts kept going over the fear of failure. "What if I mess this up?" I kept thinking. "Perhaps I bit off more than I could chew" was a thought that kept running through my mind. This was my first time trying to break seven cinder blocks. I was doing the demonstration in front of a large audience in Newport Beach, California at the Newport Beach Boys & Girls Club where I had a karate club at the time. Some of my students from my main school at the University of California, Irvine were also there to see my demo. I was putting my credibility on the line and so there was no way of turning back in my mind. Fear of the unknown started to take hold. Before long, I was focused on all the wrong things.

When it came time for me to attempt my break, I remember thinking, "Oh well, what's the worst thing that can happen? The answer: "I will look foolish and possibly break my hand." You can imagine how well my break went. My **AIM** was off as I had not properly prepared with intentionality. The good news is I did break all seven. The bad news is it took me about five tries. I ended up breaking two or three on the first attempt. Then one or two more on the second. Then it took me several more attempts to break the last one or two as my hand was nearly gelatin by that point. Lesson learned. *Where attention goes...energy flows!*

I was reminded of a powerful truth that day. That is, **you get in life whatever you focus on the most**. Stated differently, in life you get what you expect and what you accept as long as you set the **right intentions and prepare** properly. Setting the right intention upfront helps.

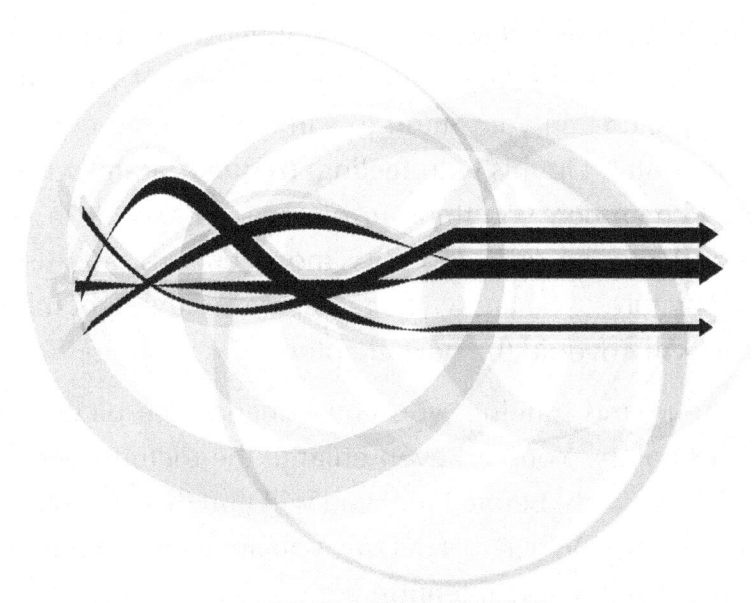

ENERGETIC DETERMINATION

Living Intentionally = Energetic Determination

You are more successful when you use your energy in a precise and positive way. For example:

1. **DIA** (Decide in Advance = setting the right intention)
2. **Have faith** (what the mind can conceive and believe it can achieve)
3. **Focus on what you want** (see it through by projecting forwards and working backwards)
4. **Be patient and persistent** (anything that is worthwhile takes a while)
5. **Value the Process** (the Master's Path is not about the destination, but rather the process)

If you find you are having a hard time harnessing the right intention or thought, start *observing* your thoughts as you observe a TV show. Be a **passive observer** at first. Identify what you *think* of the most. Then start to direct your thoughts to what you *want* the most. Use pictures in your mind to summon a more compelling vision and future. Do this with **feeling, frequency,** and with **vivid imagery.** Remember, you think in pictures and speak in words. When you have the right thoughts and intentions, and use empowering pictures, you are well on your way to the **right mindset**, which we will cover in the next chapter.

With time and training, you can enhance the pictures with more vivid colors. You can even enlarge the pictures and make them 3D if you wish. Before long, you will find that you are in fact part of the picture. When this occurs, you are well on your way to harnessing life-changing intention.

Being an expert observer requires heightened awareness. To better help you to this level, start by watching your thoughts and controlling your breath. This will also help you focus your mind and is the beginner's path to energy cultivation. As you may know, the average person has thousands of thoughts passing through their mind every day. As humans, we tend to focus or concentrate on some thoughts (mostly negative) for extended periods of time. However, most of our thoughts pass by practically unnoticed. This is why the technique I will share with you now will help you watch your thoughts while at the same time helping you cultivate energy that can propel you forward along the Master's Path:

Perform every action with <u>conscious intention</u>!

For many, the word "perfect" conjures up the idea of *being* perfect. As humans, we already know this is not possible. This said, we can always strive for *excellence.*

Remember the saying, "The little things don't mean a little... they mean a lot." If you take care of the little things, the big things will take care of themselves. It's about **being intentional about everything you do**.

Quest Challenge: Take Score

Use your journal to score yourself on the following:

1. <u>Being Intentional</u> = 10 points
2. <u>Demonstrating a positive mental attitude</u> = 5 to 10 points

Next, you might consider using the following template to better plan your week of extraordinary accomplishments. John C. Maxwell in his excellent book, <u>Living Intentionally</u>, discusses a similar template.

- <u>Sunday</u> – *Find at least one way to serve God, family, and or country. (The score should be based on the impact you made and how challenging it was.)*

- _Monday_ – Be the first to offer help.
- _Tuesday_ – Partner with a friend to make a difference.
- _Wednesday_ – Do at least one intentional act of kindness (preferably more!).
- _Thursday_ – Enjoy some intentional meal time conservation.
- _Friday_ – Surprise someone with how much they matter.
- _Saturday_ – Be intentional in planning your next week and grateful for all you have.

When the time comes to write the complete story of your life, how will it read? My hope is it will be a masterpiece. For this to happen, you must be intentional.

Chapter 3

Acting Courageously with Confidence

Intention has brought you this far in the book. But are you courageous enough to get to the very end? And, once you do, will you be confident enough to apply all that you've learned in theory throughout the book?

The **two primary components** of the Master's Path are *discipline and acting courageously with confidence.*

But what comes first – confidence or courage?

The question above is much like the question of "what comes first, the chicken or the egg?". The answer is: it takes both. You can't have a chicken without an egg. But you also can't have an egg without a chicken. It's not "either, or"; it takes both to make things happen. Similarly, it takes confidence to have courage and it takes courage to gain confidence. This said, you must <u>first exhibit courage</u> to develop confidence.

> It takes:
>
> **Desire + Courage + The Right Choices/Actions + Persistence**
>
> ...to develop **lasting confidence**

I hope you would agree that courage is something that can be developed over time. In fact, acting courageously with confidence is like planting a tree. When is the best time to plant a tree? The answer according to Darrell Putnam is:

"The best time to plant a tree is 20 years ago. The second-best time is now." – Darrell Putman

I have learned that, once the right choice is made, it often takes courage to follow through to make it happen. It often takes many tries to accomplish our biggest goals. This is why courage plus persistence are key to developing lasting confidence.

Confidence ebbs and flows over time. Circumstances often challenge our confidence and yet, at the end of the day, persistence pays off. I have also discovered that the more times I try, the more times I succeed. And, the more times I succeed, the more confident I become.

Be It Rather Than *Fake It*

We live in times where praise is often overdone. Don't get me wrong, it is a good thing to praise someone for their hard work and dedicated effort...especially if it is earned and you are sincere. Unfortunately, this has morphed over the years into something quite different. It seems today that everyone is praised for everything to help build up their self-esteem. The words "awesome", "special", and "gifted" are used to acknowledge relative normalcy. Today, people receive medals, trophies, and awards for just showing up. This can, and often does, more damage than good.

I know parents have good intentions when they over do praise and yet it seems to me that the better path when it comes to self-esteem is following the advice below:

- Praise needs **to be earned** and it needs to be legitimate.
- Praise the **process**, not the outcome.
- Praise the **behavior**, not the person.
- Praise the **positive attribute that** you want rather than giving everyone a trophy, ribbon, or medal for showing up.

Remember, if you want to build long-lasting self-esteem that doesn't disappear the first time an obstacle or failure surfaces, praise effort, attitude, discipline, persistence, and not an award that is given out freely to everyone whether they try or not. Praise what you want to last forever. Praise discipline, dedication, being respectful, loyal, humble, supportive, action-oriented, encouraging, studious, inquisitive, goal-oriented, wise, measured, passionate, purposeful, focused, patient, committed, confident and courageous to name just a few.

It is a rinse-and-repeat process. **Persistence** is needed if you aspire to excellence. One of my favorite quotes that touch on the power of persistence or perseverance is:

"I have not failed. I've just found 10,000 ways that won't work."
– Thomas Edison

Desire: An Essential Ingredient for Confidence and Courage

The first step in all achievement is desire. It doesn't matter how many times a hero falls down; he or she is always ready to get up one more time as their desire and spirit are strong. Just as weak desires bring weak results, strong desires bring strong results.

It is also important to remember that your subconscious mind works continuously. It works while you are awake and while you are asleep. It works while you are focused in and also while you are distracted. Of course, advertisers understand this and that's why they are constantly trying to trigger your deep-seated desires in the hope to get you to act and buy their products and or services.

THE TERROR BARRIER - STEPPING OUT OF YOUR COMFORT ZONE

Confronting FEAR and the Terror Barrier

"Do the thing you fear; and death of fear is certain."
– Ralph Waldo Emerson

You may be familiar with the acronym for **FEAR**. That is **F**alse **E**vidence **A**ppearing **R**eal. Of course, the evidence is not false to the person who has the fear. In this case, FEAR falls under the category of one of the universal laws…**the Law of Relativity.** That is, really, compared to what?

Let me give you an example. For one person, getting on an elevator or escalator is a fearful experience. For another, climbing El Capitan with ropes is an opportunity to live at a higher level – all puns intended. This same person might be fearful however of *free*-climbing El Capitan and yet it has been done. In this case, it is all relative.

It is important to confront the "**terror barrier**" along the path. How you perceive the challenge is a result of none other than your own programming and mental conditioning. Some welcome the terror barrier while others shy away from it – the end choice is yours, be it a conscious or unconscious one. But know this: *Your perception is your reality.* What you perceive as real is you, and no one else. Hence, changing *you* can change your reality.

I have a good friend who for years was into skydiving. In fact, he was using a wingsuit well into his sixties. Just imagine diving out of a perfectly fine airplane with nothing more than a flying suit as you propel towards earth horizontally at speeds of up to 220 mph! For most of us, the terror barrier would present itself in a major way at just the thought of the experience. I am sure it did for my friend the first time he tried it. But after many successful flights (and even one accident that put him in the hospital), he became very proficient at it and enjoyed the thrill of victory many times over – and this despite the agony of defeat after landing one time on rocks. Ouch!

Don't get me wrong. I am not suggesting you try wingsuit flying anytime soon. Your challenge or new idea may be something much tamer, much more down-to-earth (literally!), and that is okay.

Imagine this: You are called upon to present something during a very important meeting at work. Your boss, and perhaps his or her boss, are present. Even though you are comfortable with the information, you face the terror barrier, as the idea of speaking in front of key influencers instills doubt and triggers fear in your mind. Now, you are faced with a dilemma, a decision that has to be made: you can either confront your fear or live with limitations. You can either break through the barrier or turn back from what scares you. The choice is yours.

The only way to consistently break through the terror barrier is **to do the very thing that scares you most**.

Repetition is another key to success here. As stated above, it is a rinse-and-repeat process. You must continue to face your fears to eventually overcome them. This in effect desensitizes you to fear. The more times you do something that is uncomfortable, the more comfortable it becomes.

This also includes getting comfortable with failure. Don't fret though, as the most successful people on earth are also the very same people who have failed the most. An example most of us are familiar with is someone who achieves greatness in professional baseball. The batting average of a person who is inducted into the Baseball Hall of Fame is 260 to 300 plus. At 300, the batter has succeeded three times out of ten tries at the base. Doesn't sound too impressive until you consider how hard it is to get on base. The same holds true for very worthy goals and extraordinary accomplishments. If it were easy, everyone would be a major success.

The key is to **start where you are** and **set small goals** before taking action. Gain momentum and track your progress. If you do this, it will be just a matter of time before you gain proficiency at the very thing that you feared the most.

Stepping Out of Your Comfort Zone

Are you confident and courageous in taking action? If you are, remember...the biggest room in the world is the room for improvement. If not, don't fret as by the end of the journey you will be very comfortable trying new things and accomplishing extraordinary feats. That is if you say "Yes" to the journey and accept the challenge.

If you are not making the progress you'd like, it may be because your goals have not been clearly defined and you are not taking the right action for the right reasons.

Is it possible that you may be spending too much time on minor areas and not enough time in the major areas?

Is it possible that you are lying to yourself (i.e., rationalizing) so that you don't have to face reality?

Is it possible that you are accepting less than you are capable of because it is easier?

Remember, in life you get what you expect and what you accept. This is why heroes expect a lot of themselves and won't accept less.

Quest Challenge: Three Big Wins

Take a few minutes each day to review your goals for the day and make sure you are taking massive action to make them happen for the right reasons. Ask yourself, are my goals congruent with who I truly want to be? This of course begs the question, "**Who do you want to be?**"

Track your time, activities and results produced. Keeping a time log is a lot like tracking expenses. It gives you a better perspective of where you are spending your time versus where you are investing your time. Invest in your future as it will always be your best bet and pay the greatest dividends.

I would like you to list your **three big wins every day**. Start with the most important thing on your list and stay with it long enough to make a dent. Do this repeatedly over time and you will improve by as much as 2% per month or as much as 24 to 25% a year. In four years, you will have improved by approximately 100%. By then, you will have used your growth mindset to leverage your abilities and those of others and be able to make a bigger dent in the universe.

Most importantly, be honest with yourself and be congruent so that your actions match your beliefs, values, and commitments.

Habits we train are habits we gain!

Anything you do repeatedly becomes habit. Good or bad. Champions (aka mindful warriors and heroes) know that they must train their brain every day. This is why you must condition your attitude every day for making it a great day.

"If you improve the way you look at things...the things you look at will also improve!" – Author Unknown

Think how much better you would be at everything you do if you trained to act courageously with confidence in everything you attempt.

Channel Superman or Wonder Woman

Many years ago, I met a very successful entrepreneur who acted in a way that impressed me greatly. After getting to know this person better and starting to actively network with him, I learned that he actively channeled Superman. No, he couldn't leap tall buildings in a single bound or stop a train dead in its tracks. He didn't even look all that impressive physically. But he was very impressive. He was not only courageous, confident, and compelling, he was very successful and owned multiple businesses. When I asked him about his success, he shared with me that he decided to channel his hero from childhood and act as if he was Superman. This led him on a path to accelerated learning, growing, sharing, serving, leading, and inspiring. At first, I thought it a bit odd that a grown man was channeling a fictional movie and TV character from his childhood. Later, I realized the power of channeling the true greats...whether real or fictional. What you are channeling or modeling is their **attributes and behaviors**.

Remember, no one who has led a life of ease has a name worth remembering. The lives of some of the most successful people who have ever lived are woven with stories of great personal struggle. One of the qualities they all shared was purpose, passion, and perseverance. These "greats" all acted courageously with confidence even when the chips were down. It was courage and confidence that were earned the old-fashioned way. Not overnight as the newest sensation or pop star but rather one step at a time through old-fashioned hard work.

Those who walk along the Master's Path all share a relentless sense of gratitude, enthusiasm, passion, and optimism. We can all learn from and admire their seemingly endless supply of confidence and courage. Don't get me wrong, I am not suggesting that you adopt a "Pollyanna" attitude. It is one thing to be positive and look for the best in every situation. It is quite another to claim the glass is half-full when it is actually empty.

In the end, we all get what we expect and accept. Some might say we get what we deserve. The point here is that heroes make their names during difficult times by thinking smarter and working harder.

Control Your Reactions

Life is full of good times and bad times. There is a season for everything. As we learned in the last chapter, we only have control over one thing: **our own behavior** including our thoughts, words, choices, actions, and habits. Understanding this, champions or heroes choose to develop attitudes, knowledge, and skillsets that lead them in the direction they wish to go. Once they determine their path, they remain diligent and act courageously with confidence as they move forward.

Acting Courageously with Confidence

Learning to control your reactions and plan your responses is key to developing life mastery.

The truth is that most people are defeated mentally long before they are physically or spiritually defeated. By developing the confidence to act courageously, you enter a new realm of wonder, excitement, and joy.

Steve Jobs – Reality Distortion

Steve Jobs was known for what some people have defined as his "***Reality Distortion***" thinking. He often distorted popular thinking of the day by redefining what was possible. This is well documented by people who worked with Steve Jobs including his partner, Steve Wozniak.

It wasn't unusual for Steve Jobs to say something like, "Don't be afraid, you can do it." They practiced the "It's impossible unless…" mentality. Stated differently, anything is possible to the willing mind. The keyword is "will" as in willpower. A person with a strong desire, backed by indomitable spirit and willpower, that takes courageous action, is destined for success. The person who dares to do great things, will surely find success along the Master's Path.

There is no doubt that a hero's confident attitude, courageous mindset, and intentionality is the greatest contagion on a team of any size. Courageous action backed with confidence is the magic elixir.

Just Do It

"Do the thing and you will have the power"
– Ralph Waldo Emerson

The Masters Path

The law of nature basically teaches us to <u>do the thing</u> and you shall have the power. You must do the thing (the work) to have the power. You must give to get. Those who don't do the work will not have the power. It's not about luck. It is about preparation, attitude, opportunity, action, and then and only then, your results will lead to confidence.

If you want confidence, you must **take action first**. You must be willing to fall down many times. Most importantly, you must have the courage to keep getting back up. Then and only then will you develop the confidence to carry on and become a hero along the Master's Path.

Here are some helpful **tips for living courageously with confidence**:

1. Wake up every day and say "**YES**" to learning, growing, sharing, serving, leading, and inspiring.
2. Be the first to offer precise praise and compliment when it is deserved.
3. Always look for the good in yourself and others.
4. Think of what you DO want in life, not what you DON'T!
5. Always be happy and grateful for what you DO have.
6. Prepare for success NOW. (DIA = Decide in Advance)
7. Always look for and seize opportunities after exacting study to determine if it's best for you.
8. Don't be afraid to take a calculated risk.

In the next chapter, we will cover how to make a major positive impact on yourself and others.

PHASE 2
Sharing and Serving

Chapter 4

Making a Major Positive Impact

Have you ever wondered why you are here? What the meaning of life is? And what your purpose within the whole unraveling of it is? This chapter will deal with answering that exact question and thus helping you move one step closer toward life mastery.

"Why am I here?" is a question that many people ask at some point in their lives. It is a common question to ponder. It is also a critical question to ask if you aspire to become a hero. The answer, of course, depends on what you want out of life.

Why you are here is more of a choice than a destiny. It is a direct result of what you choose to do with your time, energy, and resources. Some people are focused primarily on making money, so they pursue a job that they feel will pay the most.

But what if there was more to life than just living paycheck to paycheck? If you're already a leader in your organization, you have long changed your mindset about money – perhaps, you're even still learning to. If you are yet to become a leader, this book will have you acquire a Master's mentality by the end of it.

But let's leave money aside for now. Your reason for living can be more than that. It can be family, certain relationships, building companies, living on a yacht, healing the sick, taking care of animals, inventing new technologies, eradicating war, leaving a legacy, or simply being a leader in all that you do.

I cannot tell you why you are here. But I can help you find the answer…and it involves **impact**.

Making a Major Positive Impact Sometimes Involves Risk

I had the pleasure of having a client years ago who was a neurosurgeon – let's assume his name was Joe. He was actually the chief of neurosurgery at a local hospital. His children received their black belts from me, and he was extremely interested in my peak performance coaching. He asked me if I had ever considered opening up schools to teach leadership and peak performance. I had already created a business plan to do just that and was actively teaching leadership at the main school.

Joe and I met over lunch to discuss his interest in becoming involved as an investor in what would have become a separate venture from my martial arts school. He eventually asked me if I would consider one other possible investor who owned a successful medical equipment supply company. As coincidence would have it, the individual he was asking about was already a client of ours and in fact was training with his family at the main school. Although the project never got off the ground, it was a wonderful learning experience for me as I thought at that time that the risks involved might outweigh the rewards. What I learned was that risk is relative, as are most things.

What I considered a sizeable risk at the time paled in comparison to what Joe the neurosurgeon would go through just a year later. You see, he decided to spearhead a commercial real-estate project with three or four other investors that was well over 30 million dollars. It seemed like a wise investment at the time. They were going to build a large medical building adjacent to the main hospital where Joe worked. Unfortunately, they decided to do this right before the 2007/2008 great recession. His fellow investors decided the timing was not right and pulled out at the last minute. Joe decided to push forward and guarantee the entire loan himself. The good news is that the building is magnificent. The bad news is that Joe lost his shirt, as the recession caused the commercial real estate market to go belly up at about the same time the building was finished. The building stood empty for the better part of five years. Today, the medical building is nearly fully leased and yet my client left Georgia in financial ruins many years ago.

In my experience, I have found that risk is a necessary part of every journey. The size of the risk is up to you, but unfortunately, a facet you may not have control over.

We never know what is around the next bend, or over the next hill. The *pandemic* has reminded me of this once again. The one thing I know for sure is that you can never go wrong in the long haul when you focus on what you love. There will always be ups and downs and/or challenges- you can count on it. This said, you can minimize risk when you focus on your area of expertise and are in it for the long haul.

Finding the Right Living

Making an impact starts with you and your lifestyle. Naturally, your career is a big part of that lifestyle – possibly one of the biggest pieces of the pie of life.

When you consider how much time you spend making a living, it is only wise to focus on finding the right career. One that compels you to learn, grow, share, serve, lead, and inspire. **One that creates impact.**

The hero understands that it is always better to direct their lives toward a noble purpose. It certainly is beneficial if you have a passion for it. Unfortunately, a *job* usually falls short of this. A job's main purpose is to pay bills.

A *calling*, on the other hand, compels one to make progress for the love of it. Most people who follow their passion have worked for years, sometimes without pay, in the form of an apprenticeship to learn the thing they love most.

Callings Come with Sacrifices

I moved to San Diego back in 1979 to follow *my* calling, my passion. I was not quite 20 years of age and wanted to study with the best. I had been enrolled at the University of the Pacific (U of P) in Stockton, California, and knew that I wanted something different out of life. With only a few hundred dollars in my pocket, I left U of P and took a flight to San Diego. I knew it was a risk because I only knew two people in San Diego, and they did not know I was coming.

After arriving at the San Diego airport and getting a taxi, I told the driver to go to Kwon's Karate Institute in Chula Vista.

MAKING A MAJOR POSITIVE IMPACT

The school was about five to ten miles north of the border and Tijuana, Mexico. Once there, I had hoped that Master Kwon or a senior black belt would be there to greet me. After paying the cab driver, I stepped out to find that the school was closed until five o'clock. As it was just after 12 noon, and the taxi had already left, I walked with a bag in hand to the closest motel which was about two to three miles away. It was truly a roach motel, and yet I was young, and followed my heart and my calling without a second thought.

I paid for one night and prayed that Master Kwon would be at the dojang at five o'clock when I returned. Fortunately, he was, and I will never forget his words when he saw me. He had a look of total surprise and a smile on his face and said, "What are you doing here?" That began an apprenticeship in which I earned only food money and an occasional new uniform for quite some time. As I was already a 1st-degree black belt and certified instructor, I immediately started teaching and assisting at the Chula Vista studio. Fortunately, the senior ranking black belt under Master Kwon put me up at his apartment until I could afford to go out on my own. Eventually, Master Kwon opened a second school in Mira Mesa about 30 to 40 miles north of Chula Vista. It was there that I eventually took over primary teaching responsibilities and truly earned my wings including a meager living. It was also there, with the help of several of the senior students, that we built a loft above the men's locker room. This was where I lived until which time I got married and moved into an apartment. I will never forget my Bunsen burner, futon, and one to two feet of headroom above the men's locker room. Nor will I ever forget the plastic kiddie pool and five-gallon container of water that I used daily to bathe. It was perfect. It was all I needed and even more. It was all about living the art with passion, purpose, and most of all persistence.

Why did I make the sacrifice? At that time, I had decided that I wanted to learn from the best. I knew I eventually wanted to make a major impact in the martial arts, and so I knew I needed to learn from someone who could teach me what I needed most. I had already had training to 1st Degree black belt in Philadelphia. I had always wanted to live on the west coast. In fact, I was ready to move to the West Coast the day after I graduated high school. This was my chance to get to the West Coast and follow my passion.

Turning Your Calling into a Career

In the book, *I Feel Great and You Will Too!*, Pat Croce speaks to the power of following your passion and making a major positive impact. Pat Croce had founded Sports Physical Therapists (SPT), Inc., which eventually merged with NovaCare, Inc., and eventually sold for approximately $40 million dollars. Coincidentally, he hailed from Broomall, PA, and also trained with Master Young Hyuk Kwon just as I had done years later.

Pat Croce had always thought big even as far back as his humble beginnings in Broomall. This was evidenced again when he became part-owner and President of the Philadelphia 76s basketball team. In his book, Pat Croce writes about training to black belt under Young Hyuk Kwon. He said, "Deep down, I knew how badly I needed to be instilled with discipline -to keep the devil down. First, there were the nuns and my father, and then football coaches, and then...Master Kwon." He goes on to say, "Young Hyuk Kwon was about 5 feet, 10 inches tall and built like a diamond. He looked remarkably like the late Bruce Lee. You could scratch a match on any part of him and start a fire. His head was a massive square, like the business end of a battering ram. He had an exceptionally long torso which, coupled with his incredible flexibility, enabled him to sit down, stretch his legs straight out in front of him, and then bend at the waist and actually touch his nose to his toes!"

I know firsthand that Pat Croce was not exaggerating in his book, as I too trained with Young Hyuk Kwon for years. It started in Philadelphia but would transition to San Diego and last for years. It is the story of the making of a martial artist and a life of helping others learn, grow, share, serve, lead, and inspire.

When I first arrived in Chula Vista, Master Kwon decided I would be a good sparring partner. I thought for years it had to be payback for all the trouble I gave my parents growing up. The truth is Master Kwon used me as his kicking and punching bag after most classes. You see, Master Kwon had a love of American boxing. His affinity for boxing would soon become mine. After karate class, he would tell me to remove my uniform top and put on boxing gloves. Most days, I would end up on the wall with him battering my upper torso. Back in those days I had highly conditioned abs, so I weathered the beating fairly well. That being said, Master Kwon made some of my previous training back in Philadelphia look like a picnic or a day at the beach. My previous training back in Philadelphia was very "old school" and quite rigorous, but this was a whole new level of physical discipline. This was the kind of training where one learns what they are truly capable of mentally, physically, emotionally, and most importantly, spiritually.

Master Kwon would also take us to Tijuana for the occasional tournament South of the border. We never had or used sparring gear in Philly or San Diego, and Mexico was no exception-it was always full contact. You either learned to get out of the way, block, or you got hit- and hit hard! Those were the days. It was all about the love of training and the passion to become better at the art.

Later, Master Kwon would take us to Santa Monica, LA, and Hollywood where I would eventually get to meet Chuck Norris at the LA Open. Mr. Norris had received his first-degree black belt in South Korea from Grandmaster Jae Chul Shin, the same instructor that Master Kwon and his brother trained under. I would later serve a second apprenticeship under Grandmaster Jae Chul Shin which lasted nearly 20 years. That apprenticeship focused on how to lead people as a regional director in several different regions in the United States. It was an important part of my journey. In one way it was the same as the physical training I had received from both of the Masters Kwon. You see, training in the martial arts and leadership are both about making something happen that would not have happened unless you worked at it with passion, purpose, and persistence. This is where I earned my wings, and it was a catalyst for positive change. Whether it was training, teaching, or leading, it was always about following my passion and doing the best I could with what I had. It has always been about the *journey* for me.

> **You can turn any job into a calling with enough passion and purpose**

Making a major positive impact is a matter of choice, not luck. This is why a hero identifies early in their journey what their

MAKING A MAJOR POSITIVE IMPACT

God-given talents are. They know their own strengths and weaknesses better than anyone else. They magnify the positives and shrink the negatives. They consider life one big training opportunity. They are always training to become better. They also live **intentionally** as we discussed in a previous chapter.

Finding the right livelihood and committing to it until you become great...is a lifelong journey that starts with **you**. This is why it is often said that "***The path to self-mastery starts with you and lasts a lifetime.***" I am sure you have heard the old saying, "the grass is not always greener on the other side." If you have a job and want a calling, start with cultivating the soil where you are. Plant good seed. Take the time to gain the experience needed to make a major positive impact. Make continual learning a part of your journey. Next, share what you have learned with as many people as possible. Remember, you must give to get. By helping others grow, you will grow as well. If you do this, the grass will be greener where you are and there may be no reason to go to the other side.

"You can get anything in life you want just as long as you are willing to help enough others get what they want." – Zig Ziglar

Just like tending to a garden or a piece of property, it takes consistent watering, sunshine, nutrients, and of course good fertilizer to make things grow. It also takes weed killer once and a while. Even the most beautiful garden or property has weeds from time to time. As human beings, we all have our own "weeds" to deal with. Remember, change your thinking and you change your world. It all starts with *you*.

Zooming In on the 3 Big Questions

There are three big questions to tackle as you begin to actualize your calling-turned-career:

Question #1: Who Am I?

What do you believe in? What principles do you live your life by? Who are you really? Authenticity is the key to success. Knowing oneself is job number one before trying to know and help others. What are your strengths and what areas do you need to shore up? Do you know?

Question #2: Who or What Are We?

To champion any great cause or mission, it is going to take more than you. No man or woman is an island as the old saying goes.

"The bigger your dream, the more important your team."
– Author Unknown

If you have small ordinary dreams, you only need a small ordinary team. If you have large extra-ordinary goals and dreams, you need a large extra-ordinary team. Remember, there is no legacy without many legs to do the leg work just like there is no success without a successor or successors.

If you plan on making a major positive impact, you need a leader who can articulate the vision and connect each individual's goals and aspirations to those of the team. You also need to make sure that the grand plan (the vision) connects to the mission (tactics). This includes helping everyone understand their role on the team and how their part is critical to the success of the entire enterprise. It also includes how team members will be rewarded and or recognized and most importantly how each team member is responsible to play their part. Accountability is key to success if you plan on making a major positive impact.

Quest Challenge: The 'We' Questions

Answer the following questions to better know who or what "**we**" are.

1. What do we do here?
2. Why do we exist?
3. What is our purpose?
4. Where do we fit in the world of existing options?
5. What are the core values of our group, organization, or community?

If you lead a team, group, or organization, every member of your leadership team regardless of role should be able to answer the questions above.

Question #3: What Do I/We Want?

What are your goals in life? Is it to enjoy life and be happy? I hope so. Is it to have peace of mind, good health, and to live with passion? Is it to make a major positive impact in the lives of others including your own? If so, you need to keep it simple for success and focus on the root. All growth starts with the root. In this case, knowing the root is knowing yourself and knowing what you want out of life.

In the next chapter, we will focus on being a true hero along the Master's Path. We will zoom in on how to **learn, grow, share,**

serve, lead, and inspire. We will also discuss the importance of trials and tribulations, challenges, and the occasional ordeal or crisis.

Chapter 5

Learn, Grow, Share, Serve, Lead, and Inspire

"Life begins at the end of your comfort zone." – Neale Walsh

In this chapter, I will share information and definite steps that should make your journey easier and ultimately more rewarding. I invite you to read and study this chapter carefully and consider it a call to action.

I also want to compliment you as I know you are on the right path. You are already a peak performer and as you are reading this information. Hopefully, you will not only read it but *apply* it. This is my wish for you.

Most people are not comfortable with change. This is not only normal but expected. We all have our routines and comfort zones.

I am sure you have heard the old saying, "The one thing that is constant in life is change." On the subject of change, here's what I know:

- If you change yourself but not your environment – growth will be slow and steady.
- If you change your environment but not yourself – growth will be slow and difficult.
- If you change your environment and yourself – growth will be faster and more successful.

As Robin Sharma says, "Why resist change when it's the main source of your growth?". Which beckons the question: what steps should one follow to get to full growth? And how do you know once you've reached the summit?

Six Basic Steps to Walking the Master's Path Successfully

Step 1: Start by Finding the Right Teacher (It's Not Who You Think!)

Experience is not the best teacher. Evaluated experience or **reflected-upon experience** is the best teacher. Earl Nightingale once said, "The quality of our lives is determined by the quality of the decisions we make." Decisions require thinking. Thinking requires reflection. Reflection is learning how to pause long enough to allow growth to catch up with you. The pandemic of 2019 or COVID-19 is a classic example. A huge time-out was imposed on us. It has been a major pattern interrupt that has given us the opportunity to reflect on where we are, where we have been, and where we are going. On what we want for the future.

Step 2: Use the Right Concentration - A Focused Mind

Heroes are known for concentrating their energy and efforts on exactly what they want. They are also well versed in blocking out anything that gets in the way of their focus. Most people would agree that one of the best ways to improve focus and concentration is to practice whatever you want to succeed at with maximum effort. While I would agree with the "play the game... full out" theory, I also think there is much more to it than just that. I believe that true success comes from sustained focus. It is maximum effort over the long haul.

Step 3: Seek a Higher Source - The Power of Intuition

We have all experienced times when we have had a gut or hunch about something. It is as if something is nudging you one way or the other and yet it is easy to miss if you are not tuned in. Intuition is what I call subtle life alchemy. Its magic is difficult to discern unless you are tuned into it. Intuition seems to come to you often when you are at a crossroads in your journey. You come to that fork in the road and you can either go one way or the other. Sometimes it is in connection with someone who brings you an opportunity or idea. Your intuition or sixth sense kicks in and you get a flash of inspiration or what is often referred to as a "knowing". It's as if a guardian angel is opening a door for you to see more clearly the way ahead.

> *"If prayer is you talking to God, then intuition is God talking to you."* – Wayne Dyer

Step 4: Activate the Success Cycle

The Acronym for the Success Cycle is **KASH:**

KNOWLEDGE – ATTITUDE – SKILLS – HABITS

Knowledge is activated through learning.

Ask yourself: What do you know that can bring you closer to success? How can you acquire or expand on that knowledge?

Attitude is activated through your reactions and behaviors. Your knowledge and experiences largely affect these.

Ask yourself: Has your knowledge influenced your attitude in any way? How can you improve your reactions and behaviors based on your knowledge?

Skills are activated when you put your knowledge to practice, practice, practice.

Ask yourself: How often do you hone your skills? Have they in any way helped you acquire more success in your life?

Habits are activated when your knowledge, attitude, and skills merge systematically and routinely.

Ask yourself: Have you acquired skills and knowledge that you made little to no use of? How can you start honing them starting today?

THE SUCCESS CYCLE

Activating the **Success Cycle**, as you can probably tell, is based largely on tweaking your mindset and thinking. In his classic book, *Think and Grow Rich*, Napoleon Hill discusses the premise of how thoughts are *things*. This is why in an earlier chapter, I mentioned over and over, "Do the thing and you will have the power." This concept not only applies to taking physical action but also to taking mental action. Using directed thought or what some call ***energetic determination***, one can increase the rate of thought vibration to a point that the thought becomes magnetic. Strong emotion creates a frequency that works as a catalyst for connecting to similar energy. The result of this charge is magnetic. It literally attracts thoughts on a similar frequency. It also resonates deep in the subconscious mind of those who connect to it. You might say it is "impressed" indelibly on their subconscious mind. You see this all the time with the world's best performers whether they be actors, musicians, business leaders, TV personalities, social media influencers, or politicians. Their energy transcends the specific medium they are using and is felt long after they are done with their performance and or presentation. We say they are impressive because they have impressed their energy or vibe on us. They have made a lasting connection.

Step 5: Time for Re-Programming

Paradigms and programming have enormous influence over your:

- Perception
- Creativity
- Time
- Happiness
- Effectiveness
- Productivity
- Logic
- Relationships

Paradigms help determine how we live our lives. They are mental programs that have almost exclusive control over our habitual behavior. It is important to note here that almost all behavior is habitual. We all have our routines. We do things day in and day out based on what we feel works best for us as individuals, families, and or community.

> *"We almost all tiptoe through life hoping to make it safely to death." – Earl Nightingale*

Unfortunately, for many, the source code they are using for their paradigms is faulty. That source code was written by people who weren't sure what they were doing. It would be like using a map to find a location that has not been updated in 10, 20, or 50 years. What makes this worse, is most people don't even know they are running outdated programming. They are totally unaware of what is holding them back. We see this time and time again with people who spend their entire lives trying to get ahead but are unhappy and unfulfilled. They are frustrated with the path they are on not knowing their own paradigms have set them up to fail. Their programing is in need of an upgrade.

But how do you create a different and, ultimately, better paradigm? And what can you expect once you do?

When you change the paradigm, the walls come down. The frame changes. The borders are expanded. The possibilities become endless. You see things differently as both the construct and the context change. That is, if you understand how to alter and adjust your perception to the current circumstance so that you do not dwell or become a victim to it, you will have a better chance of succeeding.

For example, as I write this chapter, we have lost the use of the internet for approximately two days. This would be devastating for many people. Now I would be lying if I told you I was happy about it when it first happened. That said, I realized that all I needed to do is look at the challenge in a different way. Instead of dwelling on the loss of my internet connection and our TV (we stream Roku, Netflix, YouTube TV, Disney +, etc.,), I could use my time to study, research, and even step away from my computer screen. I could also use the time to spend with family including our four-legged friend Mickey. I could get caught up with phone calls and or I could work out in the yard. Even better, I could take a hike and spend time in nature with loved ones. Before long, the challenge of losing the internet seemed a million miles away. What at first seemed like a major annoyance, had actually created an opportunity to explore different and potentially better paradigms. It is as if a portal opened that had always been there but was somehow shrouded by connectivity to the internet. Don't get me wrong. The worldwide web has many advantages. This said, there is a reason it is called a *web*. Much like a spider web, it is easy to get caught up in. It is easy to get stuck and eventually get lost to the outside world.

"In order to change an existing paradigm, you do not struggle to try and change the problematic model. You create a new model and make the old one obsolete." – R. Buckminster Fuller

I am reminded of a time we were in San Diego visiting family. We had decided to go out to see a movie at the local cinema plex located in an outside mall. We had purchased our tickets but the doors had not yet opened to enter the theater. As we waited, a conversation ensued between myself, my wife, and my sister-in-law who had joined us for the show. There must have been at least 20 to 30 people in line and it soon became apparent that we were the only ones speaking with each other. It also became apparent that we were the only people in line over 45 years of age. The rest of the crowd were much younger and they were all conversing as well…only they were using their smartphones to converse via texting. They were standing in line together and in many cases right next to each other and yet their connectivity was being done via data and WIFI. I share this to make a point as it relates to paradigms. We use the mode of communication that we are most familiar with and what has become habitual behavior over time. There is no doubt that technology has influenced our paradigms. In fact, I was speaking with a client the other day and she mentioned her bandwidth was limited. She wasn't talking about her high-speed fiber connectivity but rather she was trying to explain she was spread thin and felt a bit overwhelmed.

Step 6: Develop and Use Willpower

Willpower is something that is not often discussed when studying heroes or champions. I find this odd in that willpower is a necessary ingredient to becoming a success. Willpower is necessary to overcome the many obstacles that a hero must face on their journey. As you know, any great journey includes trials, tribulations, and the occasional crisis. There are always challenges and obstacles to overcome. There will always be problems as they are part of life.

The truth is the size of your accomplishments and ultimately your life will be in direct proportion to the size of your problems and your ability to solve them. Every one of us has 24/7 x 365. That is, we all have 24 hours in a day, seven days a week. We also all have 365 days in a year. It all comes down to how you use this time. Where you focus your energy and how you use your resources. This is why we will focus on goal setting in the next two chapters. You see, if you have small goals, you will get small results. Conversely, if you have large goals, you will get large results or at least larger than if you didn't stretch yourself in the first place.

"It's not whether you get knocked down, it's whether you get up." – Vince Lombardi

THE SUCCESS PARADIGM

The Master's Path – The Success Paradigm

It is time to zoom in on a paradigm that I believe will bring you extraordinary success. I believe this as it has brought me success for the past 45 years. The paradigm I am sharing is broken into three phases and encompasses a life, a lifestyle, and a legacy – you've most likely already noticed that this book is divided into these phases. This paradigm focuses on the journey through the Master's Path…and you're already on it!

The Master's Path consists of **three phases** which are the construct of success. They are:

- **Phase 1: Learn/Grow (The Memory Stage)**
- **Phase 2: Share/Serve (The Practical Application Stage)**
- **Phase 3: Lead/Inspire (The Performance Level Stage)**

Let's take a closer look at **phase one**...learning and growing including the memory stage.

Phase 1: Learn/Grow (The Memory Stage)

In Phase 1, we begin learning and growing. We go to school and learn how to interact with other people. We learn how to study and we are introduced to discipline by our parents, teachers, and coaches. This is what we call **the memory stage**. This is where our first memories are made. It is during these formative years that we form our initial paradigms and habitual habits. If we are lucky, we learn some very important lessons during phase one. We also grow as human beings. We grow both physically but more importantly, we grow mentally. It is during this phase that we learn the **six learning steps** which were introduced to me in a seminar I did with Grandmaster Andy Ahpo. They are:

1. **Look** with the intent to learn
2. **Listen** with the intent to learn
3. **Record** and **visualize**
4. **Imitate** what you see
5. **Practice**, practice, and practice some more
6. **Rinse, repeat,** and **develop** creativity as you grow

As you have probably noticed by now, your greatest teacher will always be life itself. You are learning how to become a peak performer by participating in life. Call them life lessons, lessons in mindfulness, challenges, or failing forward, it is all about learning and growing. The lessons are learned as you take your journey... as you walk the path. The goal is to enjoy life and make a difference along the way. It is about being congruent as you walk your talk and contribute to the greater good.

However, **growth is not a single event**. Rather, it is a series of lessons learned along the way. It also takes time and persistence – so it's not a quick fix to your problems. Some lessons can even be quite painful or difficult to accept. But this type of learning is superior as it is cumulative. We learn, we apply, we overcome, and we repeat. We do this in many different ways as we take the journey. Over time it has a compound effect and you gain wisdom if you learn from your mistakes.

It is during Phase 1 that you meet your mentors or guides. They are your parents, teachers, coaches, and select friends. It is during this time that you are introduced to new ideas, opportunities, and experiences. You attend different events and make new distinctions. It is during this phase that you learn the necessary skills to move forward. You also learn the importance of repetition. You learn it over and over until it is internalized.

During this phase, you learn how to step out of your comfort zone and take a chance. Think of your younger years: whether it was riding a bike, a motorcycle, or driving a car, you learned there were certain rules of the road you must know and pay attention to. You also learned there was the risk of failure and tests or challenges along the way. Whether they were tests in school, with relationships, or on your first job, you learned that the one thing that is constant throughout life is **change**.

For me, Phase 1 was kicked into high gear in the summer of 1976. I was 15 years of age and about to turn sweet 16. My uncle, aunt, and cousins lived in Hanau, Germany, on the Pioneer Kaserne or army base. My parents had decided I needed a change of scenery from what would have been just another summer of hanging out with my friends. Our greatest challenge during the summer was that we had too much time on our hands.

I will never forget my first ever airplane ride or flight from Philadelphia to Frankfurt, West Germany. This was before the wall came down and so Germany was still divided into east and west. I had never been out of the country and so this was an experience that was sure to open my eyes and especially my mind.

I had always been close with my cousins. They had lived not far from us in New Jersey before moving to Germany. I had spent a good deal of time with them both prior to the trip. My cousin Linda was four years older and Bob was almost a year older than me. Both Bob and I had a love for music and especially guitars… we still do. That bond was cemented even further during the summer as we hitchhiked and backpacked throughout Europe. From Frankfurt to Amsterdam and Zandvoort in the Netherlands, to eventually Austria, Switzerland, and Italy we traveled all summer long. I will never forget the people we met along the way. They impressed me with their knowledge and especially their hospitality. One such example was two Frenchmen (Jerome and Thibou) and their female friend (Chantelle) we met when hitchhiking through Holland. Once we left Amsterdam, we all headed to the North Sea and a small resort community called Zandvoort. It was on the beach that Jerome and Thibou taught me the basics of Savate or French kickboxing. I will also never forget meeting Steve and Miki in Bavaria about a month later as we sat down to a lunch of cheese and bread at the foot of Neuschwanstein Castle just outside of Fussen. Miki was Japanese. They were backpacking through Europe as well.

The summer of 1976 was the essence of growth as not a single event but rather a series of learning experiences. It was not only the change of scenery and the different cultures but the experiencing of hardships along the way that shaped me that summer and well beyond. For example, I learned what it was like to get stuck on the side of a freeway offramp along the autobahn for the better part of a day without food. Fortunately, someone had the heart to eventually pick us up despite what we looked like at the time. As it turned out, the fellow who picked us up could tell we were in need of food and drink and drove us to his small town for coffee and snacks. He also gave us a quick tour and showed us some of the sites in this most picturesque cobble-stoned village. I was learning what life was like in other parts of the world. I was also growing through experiences that only come with actively taking the journey. Most importantly, it opened my mind to all the possibilities.

Towards the end of the summer, Linda, Bob, myself, and one other friend decided to treat ourselves to just under a week in Lloret de Mar, Spain. We flew to Barcelona and took a bus to the Costa Del Brava. The resort community was a hot spot for British tourists and the Flamenco dancing and sangria were second to none (or at least that was how I saw it at the time).

When I returned home, I was not the same person who left three months earlier. I had a new sense of purpose and a new-found passion to learn, grow, and to one day travel the world and experience other places and cultures. I had just turned 16 years of age but knew I wanted more than a comfort zone. I wanted to explore and see and experience new places. I had set big goals for myself. I wanted to study history, different cultures, esoteric philosophies, music, architecture, and most of all the martial arts. It was all possible and it still is. The only thing that has changed is my perspective on how I see these things. My paradigms have changed over time. I started to see how by sharing and serving, I could reach my goals more quickly. I was ready for Phase 2 - the practical application stage.

> *"When you affirm big, believe big, and pray big, big things happen." – Norman Vincent Peale*

Phase 2: Share/Serve (The Practical Application Stage)

I had stated in an earlier chapter that you can get anything in life just as long as you are willing to help enough other people get what they want. The practical application of the philosophy is what all heroes are about. They are about **sharing and serving at a higher level**. This of course requires more learning and growing and also the desire and decision to serve an apprenticeship. To apply your knowledge and skills while serving others. I truly believe the purpose of human life is to serve, and to do this all you need to do is share with passion and compassion.

I had mentioned that in Phase 1 you meet your guides and or mentors. In Phase 2, you learn that, if you want to make a real difference in the lives of others, you have to find a different type of guide or mentor. This is where you seek out an expert in the field you are interested in and study with someone who has walked the specific path you intend to take. In Phase 2, you look for a specialist and model their mindset, behaviors, and strategy.

What I learned during Phase 2 is how important it is to *internalize* the knowledge, skill sets, and attitude needed to perform at a high level. I learned the best way to do this was to teach the very thing I needed most. I knew from guides and mentors that it was only by teaching others, by sharing my knowledge and skills, that I could grow as a mentor, guide, coach, and or teacher. I learned it was more about application in Phase 2, whereas Phase 1 was more about education. Don't get me wrong, I was still focused on my education, and in fact was still working on my college degree. The difference was now I had to also consider the best way to educate my students as I was teaching karate while attending college. This required more advanced skills such as planning, promotion, public speaking, writing, and creating curriculum and lesson plans in addition to handling my college course load.

"Far and away the best prize that life offers is the chance to work hard at work worth doing." – Theodore Roosevelt

Phase 3: Lead/Inspire (The Performance Level Stage)

This phase is **where mastery resides**. It is where one becomes a total practitioner of their art. It is what we refer to as "Mushin" or the mind no-mind state. This is where you have transcended your practice to a place of unconscious competence. You have grown through many years of practice to a place where you can perform at a very high level without thought or preparation. This is what many call being in the zone.

In his book, *Outliers*, Malcolm Gladwell talks about the number of hours of practice it takes to master something. He suggests that one needs at least 10,000 hours of practice. I am not sure if this number is correct but I can tell you from experience that **it takes as long as it takes.**

Learn, Grow, Share, Serve, Lead, and Inspire

You will remember earlier that I said heroes see their walk as a sacred mission. Their purpose and passion are so strong that nothing can deter them from their destiny. This is the power of performance level. A true artist will perform because they need to. Yes, they want to but not for money or fame, although that is not necessarily a bad thing. They want to because it is their identity. It is who they are. It is what they are all about. No matter what obstacles they face, they carry on as they realize that nothing worthwhile comes easily. It is mostly all uphill. If you want to reach the summit, you have to be able to climb. You can't wait for the spirit to move you. **You have to create the spirit.**

YOUR SACRED MISSION

"The man who has attained mastery of an art reveals it in his every action." – Samurai Maxim

Before concluding this chapter, I would like to leave you with a few simple thoughts to help recap the **Success Cycle** and **Success Paradigm**. They are:

- **Build and develop yourself first** before trying to build and develop others. (The Law of the Lid)
- You must **give to get**. You must also **give to grow**.
- **Serve** where you are needed most.
- Remember, you are in the people business or "H2H" which is **"human to human"**.
- **Help change lives** for the better one person at a time.

THE LAW OF THE LID

We will be covering leadership and inspiration at a much deeper level as we continue our journey. For now, let me say that the future belongs to those who can lead successfully.

"Everything rises and falls on leadership." John C. Maxwell

Quest Challenge: Your Success Paradigm

Before leaving this chapter, take the time to honestly answer the following questions in your journal:

1. Do you know what paradigm or paradigms are driving your habitual behavior?
2. Are your habitual behaviors congruent with your core values? If not, why not?
3. What three extraordinary things do you plan to accomplish this year?
4. Do you have specific goals written down to achieve these goals?
5. How can you apply what you have learned in this chapter to your life?

In the next chapter, we will focus on four key core competencies of **Leadership**.

Chapter 6

Leadership Core Competencies

"The true measure of leadership is influence – nothing more, nothing less." – John C. Maxwell

Becoming a modern leader might be one of the most important things you will ever do. No doubt, becoming a current leader will help you in every area of your life. As stated earlier, great leaders will always be in demand. A person who can build confidence and strength in others is rare indeed. This is especially true if they can also inspire hope and mobilize others to act.

In this chapter, you will learn the core competencies needed to lead others effectively. We will review key concepts and strategies that will help you become a more effective leader. To accomplish this, we will cover four primary areas of focus. They are:

1. Building Confidence and Strengths in Others
2. Inspiring Hope and Mobilizing Others to Act

3. Connecting Emotionally with Others
4. Attracting and Captivating Others

As this is no small order, we will cover some of these topics in more depth in future chapters. Hopefully, this will help you internalize the lessons better and help you gain new perspectives as you continue your journey along the Master's Path.

Building Confidence & Strengths in Others

All leaders are in the people business. So this is the good news and the bad news. Let me explain. Human beings are a very complex species. To lead effectively, you have to become proficient in both human nature and human relations, so it is essential to know *yourself* before trying to help others. You have to be able to lead yourself before you can hope to lead others effectively.

Leadership is truly an inside job. It requires that you understand what makes people tick. Ultimately, it starts with you and *then* those you hope to lead.

The **three types of leaders** are:

- Those that watch what happened
- Those that wonder what happened
- Those that make things happen

You may recall that I mentioned earlier that the best way to learn how to lead is to study with someone who is already an effective leader. This is the **Law of Modeling**. It's hard to improve when you have no one but yourself to follow, as the old saying goes. The truth is you need to develop the skills of modern leadership through practice. No different than anything else you intend to master.

Just as you need to know your strengths, weaknesses, and interests to grow yourself, you need to know your team members' strengths, weaknesses, and interests to be able to grow them. It requires the ability to build rapport and connect with others. It requires that you take a genuine interest in those you hope to lead. It requires heightened awareness on your part and the ability to ask good questions. It also requires the ability to listen effectively and then set goals to help your team members to get from where they are – to where they want to be. No easy task, and yet it all starts with <u>you</u> and a genuine interest in building others' confidence and strengths.

If I have learned anything in the 40-plus years I have been leading others, it is never to *assume* someone is confident. Just because someone is projecting confidence doesn't mean that they are. The truth is that people often suffer from what some call the "**Imposter Syndrome.**" That is, they don't believe they are worthy of their position at a subconscious level. In this case, they may have a leadership position, but they are still genuinely trying to lead themselves. I see this often with those who are new in their leadership role. It was no different for me when I first started in a leadership position. Whether it was my first school, my first management position with State Farm Insurance, or my first time being the head of an international organization. As I said in a previous chapter, "all winners start as beginners."

In his books, *The E-Myth* and *The E-Myth Revisited*, Michael Gerber addresses the difference between the Technician, the Manager, and the Entrepreneur or Leader. The **Technicians**, especially those who are talented, love doing what they do best. Work is their comfort zone. In a factory, these are the lead workers who love building widgets or whatever product is sold. The **Manager** is the individual who oversees the process. They, in effect, manage the work. The **Entrepreneur/Leader** is the person who first became the Technician and then the Manager, but was able to grow to a much bigger role. While Managers manage the process, leaders lead people. Entrepreneurs start and create businesses and need to know how to lead people to run a successful enterprise. The most successful Entrepreneurs and Leaders often replace themselves, so they are free to start new businesses or enterprises and lead more people.

20th Century Leadership vs. Modern Leadership

For those of us who were raised during the great generation or the baby boom, we learned a very top-down leadership style and hierarchal approach.

Those who were raised in these generations were indoctrinated with the following **beliefs**:

- Work hard, and someday you may get a raise.
- Pay your dues and bide your time, and it will pay in the end.
- Good things come to those who wait.
- Keep your nose to the grindstone, and someday your efforts will bear fruit.

While these traits can serve the greater good, it is important to note that modern leadership is focused more on collaboration and less on hierarchy. Patience is still important, and yet time is seen differently in the 21st century. Technology has compressed time. In the 21st century, it's not more time but more intensity. In this case, intensity is a function of using technological leverage. Good leaders understand this and therefore provide clarity early on during the onboarding process to better collaborate with their team members. Successful leaders not only collaborate but also lead through **facilitated introspection**.

Facilitated introspection is not about telling someone what to do but rather about finding their way and learning from their mistakes. This is done by asking better questions. Successful leaders understand the best way to help a person discover their fullest potential is to help them learn from experience. This discovery process allows the person to find the hidden power locked up in their psyche. This takes a bit more time but is much more effective in creating positive lasting change. It increases awareness (both self-awareness and situational awareness) and ultimately leads to a better understanding, better relationships, and a better work environment. It also helps build trust as it requires honesty and vulnerability, which helps each party better understand the other's emotional state. As we are all emotional beings, successful leaders use this technique very effectively to build a connection between themselves and their team members.

Successful Traits That Lead to Effective Leadership

What follows are **success traits** practiced by 21st-century leaders to help build confidence and strength in others:

1. **Happy but not satisfied.** There is an old Zen proverb that says, "Before enlightenment – chop wood and carry water; after enlightenment – chop wood and carry water." This can be interpreted to mean that one should have a goal, to be constantly striving toward better, but not to concentrate so much on the goal that you forget the path. Successful leaders help their team members to understand that life is

truly a journey. This is why they focus on effort first and foremost.

2. **Compare yourself not to others, but to your own potential.** When you compare yourself to others, you are missing the mark. There is always someone who will be better than you at a particular thing. Comparing team members to each other leads to people feeling either incompetent or overconfident. Not everyone is equal in knowledge, skill, attitude, and habits. Successful leaders understand that the best way to build confidence and strength in others is to help their team members develop their own potential. They do this by helping each individual set realistic goals that help achieve the enterprise's sacred mission while helping the team member grow and become more valuable.

3. **Create small wins.** Having high expectations is not an issue unless your expectations are out of whack with the team member's ability. Successful leaders help their charges create small wins to build momentum. Once momentum is created, they help their team members set bigger goals with higher expectations. This helps create a **self-fulfilling prophecy**. If the team member genuinely believes you have their best interest at heart, they will work harder to reach their fullest potential. Remember, people don't lack potential. They only lack a good leader: someone who believes in them. It is the belief and confidence of the leader that lifts us from ordinary to **extraordinary**. Successful leaders do this by starting with small wins. By doing this, they help build confidence. It's about getting some wins or "W's" early and often. This leads to building confidence and, with time, the team member's indomitable spirit. As

victories mount, team members experience the winner's effect or power of momentum.

4. **Successful leaders praise.** Successful leaders recognize personal and team victories. They do this by spotlighting and highlighting accomplishments in team meetings and on recognition boards. Successful leaders understand that people will work hard for the money but even harder for recognition. If you want to build someone's confidence truly, you should start by letting them know how much you appreciate their efforts. The only caveat, as mentioned in an earlier chapter, is to be specific when complimenting your team member. Saying "good job" is not specific enough. Tell them what you appreciate specifically.

5. **Successful leaders see problems as opportunities.** One of the best ways to help your team members is to reinforce the idea that problems are nothing more than opportunities in disguise. A problem is nothing more than a challenge looking for a solution. The most successful leaders see problems differently than most people. They see opportunities where others see insurmountable obstacles. Successful leaders let their employees figure things out on their own, as this is always the best way to learn. It also strengthens their resolve for the next time a problem might be encountered. This is why good leaders never tell their charges how to do things. Instead, they tell them what to do and let them figure it out on their own from there.

6. **Successful leaders listen.** leaders understand that their team members will tell them everything they need to know if given the right opportunity. This is why they ask good questions and listen carefully to the responses. They also

take good notes and summarize their understanding of the comments made. They have learned that silence is truly golden. While most people are already thinking about what they are going to say next, successful leaders are very different. They know that listening effectively is the quickest way to uncover what is going on inside the minds of their team members. We will cover listening in much more detail in the next chapter.

Inspiring Hope & Mobilizing Others to Act

I was blessed to have found an opportunity to work with an excellent boss and leader at State Farm's Insurance Corporate Headquarters in Bloomington, Illinois. I will never forget working for "David." He inspired hope and allowed me to fail forward once again. David was so positive. I also know he believed in me as he told me so. He trusted me to do my job, and it was right up my alley. My position was about motivating managers and helping them to empower their employees. As part of this job, I was required to write training manuals and present seminars to managers who were sent to corporate for different specialized programs. This was truly the next phase of the hero's journey along the Master's Path.

David was the type of leader and boss that understood the concept of teamwork. He inspired each of us to give our best but let us figure out the best way to do that. It was not unusual for him to welcome me into his office to just chat about life in general. I felt that David was my friend and truly cared about my progress. He inspired hope in me and taught me several very important lessons that, to this day, I will never forget. David was a genuinely nice person who truly cared about his employees. He was knowledgeable, easy-going, and helped reinforce our mission. He mobilized all of his analysts under a common cause that we worked very hard to achieve. He was all about excellence. He also believed very strongly that it took a team even though he treated us very much as individuals.

I was fortunate that David was also my neighbor. My wife and I were fortunate to have sold our very first home in Southern California for a sizeable profit and decided to reinvest our equity in a fairly large home in Bloomington. Little did we know when we bought the house that my boss was one of my neighbors. What really surprised us, however, was that our property adjoined a rather large farm owned by the President, CEO, and Chairman of the Board of State Farm Insurance. We found this out the day we moved in as we were unloading empty boxes out on our back deck. My wife and I glanced over, and there he was, fixing his fence about 40 feet from our deck. It was Mr. Rust, the president and CEO of State Farm Insurance, waving hello. I came to learn that Mr. Rust, and his father (the previous President and CEO of State Farm) were accomplished at much more than insurance. This became apparent when I saw the size of his machine shop where he made parts for his various farm implements and commercial grade earth-moving equipment.

The real lesson came about six months after moving into our new home. It was from this experience that I truly learned how great leaders think and act. I am sure you have heard the acronym for **TEAM** is "*Together Everyone Achieves More.*" What I didn't realize was that great leaders live this concept. You see, Mr. Rust's property, as large as it was, would accumulate substantial amounts of water in the torrential downpours so common in the corn belt of central Illinois. When it rained hard, the swell on his property would send large volumes of water onto not only our property but several of the homes that backed up to his fence. This was only a small annoyance for us, but several of our neighbors had flooding in their basements as a result of the issue.

I had decided to talk to David about it and get his thoughts. I will never forget him counseling me to tread carefully as Mr. Rust, was his boss's, boss's, boss's boss. You can imagine the pickle we were in. How do you contact the president and CEO of the company you work for and let him know he needs to fix his drainage problem, which has become *your* drainage problem? After much thought and a good deal of worrying, I spoke with my neighbors, and we decided to contact both the builder and the developer of our sub-division. My hope was we could handle it without getting Mr. Rust involved.

The Difference Between World Class and the Masses

As a result of our contact with a city official, the builder, developer, and the neighbors were given an opportunity to discuss our concerns in person at a meeting to take place at the local county office where all parties would meet to discuss the best way to resolve the problem. What I didn't expect was Mr. Rust, would be there as well.

The day came for the big meeting. After everyone took their seats, Mr. Rust walked in and nodded to us all as he took a seat. We sat through about ten minutes of both the builder and the developer saying it was not their responsibility and that we would have to fix it ourselves. I remember expressing my concern and stating that the problem was the result of improper grading. One of my neighbors had expressed the flooding was causing his basement to flood. It was apparent that we were at an impasse. That was until Mr. Rust stood up and walked to the front of the room and approached a whiteboard that was attached to the wall. It was then that I learned how great leaders handle problems.

Mr. Rust told everyone that after listening to the concerns, it was apparent to him that his property was the proximate cause of the drainage issue. He then used a dry erase marker to diagram how it could easily be fixed. It went something like this. He said, "I will take my tractor and bulldozer and move enough dirt to create a proper berm. I will then redirect overflow water by putting in a French drainage tile or pipe, and I would like my neighbors to tie it into it. Of course, I will be happy to help them if they need an extra hand. I want the builder and or developer to contact their grading company and make sure that drainage pipe is brought from the neighbor's backyards where they tie into the front curb at no cost to them as I do believe the backyards in question were improperly graded." He then went on to say, "This will get excess water to the storm drains out at the curb." What he said next I will never forget. He said, "Do we have any questions?" and put down his marker. He then said, "I have always believed that working as a team is the best solution." He talked for less than five minutes. He was clear, caring, and to the point. Everyone present, including the builder and developer, was nodding in agreement. The only thing missing at the end of his talk was all of us saying, "yes, sir." Mr. Rust was not only decisive. He was genuine. He had provided a solution and was willing to back it up with action. His credibility spoke volumes. By the way, his part of the agreement was done within days of our meeting. He completed his end of the bargain himself. I saw him outside on his Caterpillar tractor in his work jeans and his old work shirt. He created the berm and laid the drain tile and pipe just as he had promised. The builder and developer had the grading company out in short order as well at no cost to the residents. I am sure it didn't hurt that Mr. Rust's company-owned most of Bloomington, Illinois. This said you would have never known it by the way he dressed outside of work. Oftentimes he was working on his farm in his work jeans and or overalls. He drove an old pick-up just as his father had before him. By the way, his grandfather, Adlai H. Rust, was also a President and CEO of State Farm Insurance before his father. You might say greatness ran in the family. You won't be surprised to learn that Mr. Rust built most of his own house on the family farm. He put his driveway in himself, which ran right next to our property. He was truly a "good neighbor" and lived the sacred mission of the company he ran. He was authentic through and through. He put meaning to State Farm's brand. That is, "Like a good neighbor, State Farm is there."

"It's not the position that makes the leader; it's the leader that makes the position." – Stanley Huffy

The Moral of One Good Story

Successful leaders give their people hope. They treat their work and their life as a sacred mission. They stand up for the small guy and truly believe that together everyone achieves more. If they have an enemy, it is indifference, intolerance, and inaction.

Great leaders inspire others by their actions, not their words. The truth is that Mr. Rust was president and CEO of State Farm not for his speaking ability but rather for his character. People knew that when Mr. Rust said he would do something, you could take it to the bank. His word was his bond. He was not only congruent in all that he did. He was decisive, sincere, action-oriented, and a world-class problem solver. He was a leader but also a team player. He was always willing to right a wrong even with those who were less important and or less well-positioned.

It would have been easy to pre-judge and make assumptions about Mr. Rust, based on what he wore around his house or even how he sometimes looked outside of work. Mr. Rust epitomized the old saying, "you can't judge a book by its cover."

Connecting Emotionally with Others

Understanding how to connect emotionally with others is pivotal in succeeding in leadership. And unless you know what people want most from their leaders, you can't be one and serve them effectively. If you demonstrate this characteristic, you will begin to grow your ability to connect and influence others. The keywords are *connect* and *influence.* The key characteristic that bridges the two is **authenticity**.

Step 1 in Connecting: Authenticity

Unfortunately, too many people hide behind a mask. They have their public persona, and it is not congruent with their true self. Let's be honest. If you are a human being, you are flawed. This said, if you want to connect emotionally with others, you need to be **real and authentic**. I am reminded of Winston Churchill when I think of authenticity. He was beloved for all his flaws. This was because he never forgot he was also human. He was not afraid to show his humanity. Agree or disagree with his wit or quips. There is no doubt he was deeply loved and respected by many throughout the British Commonwealth.

Winston Churchill was one of the most influential figures in British history. He proved you don't have to be a motivational speaker to connect emotionally with others. He also wasn't afraid to tell people exactly how he felt. The key to his success, other than his confidence and courage, was that he was authentic. He connected with people on a very visceral level. He did this by giving the public a sober assessment of the situation during World War II and then laid out logical reasons for how and, most importantly, *why* they would overcome the enemy. In this case, Nazi Germany was the enemy, and he gave the British people hope that they could win the war even though the Nazis were in the midst of some of the most intense aerial bombings anyone could imagine at that time. He was able to rally not only the troops but also the masses because they believed in this great man and what he had to say. His call to action was we will fight, and we will not give up. His authenticity, combined with his indomitable spirit, was precisely what the British needed at that time in history. His ability to connect and influence people was not only real it was very powerful.

Step 2 in Connecting: Vulnerability

To connect emotionally with others, you need to be more than courageous and confident. You also need to be **vulnerable**. You cannot lead for long by command alone. You have to lead by opening yourself up and showing your humanity. Everybody is eager to share what is beautiful, powerful, and or incredible. This said, if you really want to connect with others, let them feel your heart, and you will touch them emotionally. Remove the armor and the mask. By doing this, you become vulnerable: something that real people can identify with.

"Leaders touch the heart before they ask for a hand."
– Author Unknown

Step 3 in Connecting: Relatability

If you want to connect emotionally with others, be **relatable**. To relate effectively, you must find common ground. This requires that you learn how to relate to people not just as a group but as individuals. The stronger the relationship and connection between individuals, the more likely they will want to help each other. This requires honesty and understanding. The truth is that we communicate with feelings, not words. Real connection touches our soul. You feel it not only in your gut but, most importantly, in your heart.

Step 4 in Connecting: Be Caring and Congruent

I am sure we have all heard the saying, "people don't care how much you know until they know how much you care." Someone who cares, truly cares, is someone who is on the Master's Path. Being **caring and congruent** makes one truly a hero.

Step 5 in Connecting: Be Resolute

Successful leaders are able to connect and influence others because they are purposeful and determined. They are **resolute**. They don't give up. Instead, they stand up for those who need their help. This requires not only a genuine interest in others but the willingness to fight injustice and or right a wrong. It requires genuine empathy and yet steadfastness of purpose. A dogged determination to do whatever is necessary to make a real difference—someone who will stand up for what is right. A leader like this can easily connect and influence others because their commitment and dedication demonstrate their character. Names like Martin Luther King, Nelson Mandela, and Mahatma Gandhi come to mind.

Step 6 in Connecting: Be Trustworthy

To be able to connect and influence others effectively, you need to be **trustworthy**. Trust is the foundation of leadership. To build trust, a leader must exhibit **three qualities**. They are:

1. Competence
2. Connection
3. Character

Competence comes from years of experience and training. It can't be faked. You either have the knowledge and ability, or you don't. It requires that you have put in the time, energy, and resources to develop the skill set necessary to demonstrate proficiency at what you are doing. We have already reviewed what it takes to make a solid **connection** with others. **Character** is covered in-depth in the next section. For now, just know that character communicates your awareness and your potential. It also communicates respect. A person of character is respected for their decision-making ability and, most importantly, their actions.

> *"The only thing that walks back from the tomb with the mourners and refuses to be buried in the character of a man. This is true. What a man is survives him. It can never be buried."*
> – J. R. Miller

Attracting and Captivating Others

In the final section of this chapter, we will cover a topic that should be very important to anyone in a leadership position. This is especially true if you are in the people business, and since all businesses involve people, this section is especially important to your success.

This section will briefly touch on ways to **captivate, attract, and persuade others**.

To start, imagine a pyramid structure, just like the great pyramid in Giza in Egypt. There is no doubt that pyramids like the longstanding ones in Egypt are solid. They are, in fact, rock-solid. They have stood the test of time and will continue to impress those lucky enough to see them in person for many generations to come. Of course, the great blocks of stone used to construct the pyramids had to be cut and shaped by master stone cutters before being placed. They had to be laid in such a way to create a foundation that would last for thousands of years. It took years to complete and thousands of specialists to create such a magnificent edifice.

After the foundation was in place, master builders had to carefully cut and lay each level of rock in succession to build the superstructure that we all know today. Each layer or level was built upon the one before it, and it required careful planning, production, supervision, and ultimately a big enough why to be able to attract and captivate others to want to work their entire lives and, in many cases, give their lives to the cause.

Similarly, if you consider a diamond in the rough, it is nothing more than a rock. It takes a master diamond cutter to give it shape. At first glance, it is flawed, and hard to see its true value. It isn't until the master cutter does the work of creating the sharp angles and edges that we start to see the brilliance of the diamond. It is the depth of the cuts and the way that light catches the edges that catches our eye. It is the sparkle that only comes after much work and careful planning that we see the true value of the diamond.

I will give you one more example. Consider how a priceless samurai sword is created. A master swordsmith must follow a very careful multi-step process that includes using high-quality steel, which is repeatedly heated, hammered flat, and then folded. This process is done to eliminate any blade-weakening air bubbles that get into the steel during the heating process. Also, the process creates layers in the metal, which adds to the blade's strength and ultimately gives the blade the look and character of being made by a master craftsman.

Whether we are talking about the construct of the pyramid, a diamond, or a samurai sword, it is a wonderful metaphor for what it takes to attract and captivate others. You see, your character must be crafted and built by a process that requires time, energy, and resources.

If the bedrock of connecting and influencing is authenticity, then the keystone of attracting and captivating others is **character**. To be even more specific, **character is job # 1**.

Think about your favorite superhero movie character. Or, if you prefer, your favorite characters in a book. We don't fall in love with the stories, we fall in love with the characters in the story. They are the heroes who stand up for what they believe in – and possibly even mirror what *we* believe in, too. The character may be someone as flawed as Bilbo Baggins of Hobbit fame or as incredible as Superman or Wonder Woman. They may have superhero qualities, but they all are slightly flawed. Even Superman has his kryptonite. Bilbo hates adventure when he first starts out. Wonder Woman has her many trials and tribulations as a young

LEADERSHIP CORE COMPETENCIES

girl and then woman. The story is about these characters overcoming their trials and tribulations and eventually overcoming their doubt, fear, and or the arch-enemy who poses a great threat. I am reminded of the great western movie Tombstone when Wyatt Earp, played by Kurt Russell, has to face members of an outlaw gang known to wear red sashes called the Cowboys, led by "Curly Bill" Brocius. There is a part in the movie where Wyatt Earp has to face Johnny Ringo in a gun battle. He knows he can't beat Johnny Ringo, but he shows up nonetheless. Fortunately for Wyatt Earp, Doc Holiday, played by Val Kilmer, is there to save the day and guns down Johnny Ringo to save his friend Wyatt.

The point here is that **we all have fears and doubts**, even our greatest heroes. We are all a bit unsure of ourselves. We all feel awkward and doubt ourselves at times. Of course, the reason for this is our ego fears that if others know our flaws, weaknesses, and insecurities, it will keep them from liking or accepting us. Or perhaps we fear not looking important. Just the opposite is true. However, it makes us more human and relatable when our imperfections are visible. The very thing that we seek to hide and or protect is the very thing that gives a diamond its radiance and sparkle. It is the sharp edges and cuts that make the polish and luster more impressive.

In any hero's journey, especially when it comes to leadership, you are going to make mistakes. Apologize and get over them. You are human. Trust me. You will make many mistakes along the way. Typically, these lessons are what build character as long as you are willing to learn from them and move on.

As we finish this chapter, I will leave you with a tried-and-true 5 step method to attract rather than alienate. To captivate rather than repel. To build rather than destroy.

5 Step Process for Attracting and Captivating

1. **Find common ground** by building rapport.
2. **Be a good finder**. Compliment sincerely.
3. **Share as opposed to selling**. Let your story attract and captivate.
4. **Invite people to join** you on the journey.
5. **Build your character.** Plant your flag! Stake your claim and stick with it.

Quest Challenge: Honest Answers

Take time to answer the following questions honestly.

1. What were the top three ideas that stood out to you in this chapter?
2. What skills do you need to improve to build confidence and strengths in others better?
3. What inspires you most? Why?
4. What are the three main considerations in inspiring and mobilizing others?
5. What do you feel is the most important factor in connecting emotionally with others?
6. How do you want to be remembered?

In Chapter 7, we will shift our focus to **Strategic Planning and Warrior Tactics**.

Chapter 7

Mastering Strategic Planning and Warrior Tactics

This chapter is full of essential things you need to consider as you continue your hero's journey along the Master's Path. The most important is, to *begin with the end in mind.* This chapter will also illuminate the steps and methods you can use to reveal your destiny, much like that of a true master warrior.

Revealing Your Legacy

If you could write your life story, how would it go? If someone was reading your biography, what would it tell them about your life?

Start by asking yourself how do you want to matter? What will your life stand for? If you're going to make a significant impact, take time now to answer the following questions:

- Why do I exist?
- What is the purpose I want to fulfill?

- What is the objective of my heroic journey?
- Why will the world be better thanks to my existence?

I know these are heavy-duty questions. Most people will never take the time to contemplate these truly. Even fewer will act upon them. As one of my mentors once said, "Everyone starts but only a few finish, and even fewer finish well." If you intend to finish well, NOW is the time to pause and reflect on these transformational questions.

Take the time to consider one more important question as we start this section of our journey. What are <u>three main things</u> you want to be said in your eulogy about who you were and how you lived?

I am reminded of a great line in the movie "*The Last Samurai,*" where the Japanese emperor asks Tom Cruise's character (Captain Algren) to tell him how the great samurai leader Katsumoto played by Ken Watanabe, died. Algren says, "I won't tell you how he died, but I will tell you how he lived." How do you plan to live? By what design do you plan on achieving greatness?

In the same movie, Katsumoto, while still living, said to Algren, "You believe a man can change his destiny?" Algren states, "I think a man does what he can until his destiny is revealed."

Here's a significant clue. Warriors like Katsumoto and Captain Algren were very aware of their environment. They planned for engagement well in advance. They continually demonstrated something the masses fail to. They anticipate and prepare for *what is next*. They also did what they could to create the life they wanted for themselves. They lived by a code and a creed. They were principled.

Mastering Strategic Planning and Warrior Tactics

This requires **strategic planning** and **warrior tactics**. It also requires awareness, discipline, and a good deal of courage and character.

Creating your Destiny with a Sacred Mission Statement

There are five things to consider as you create your destiny. They are:

1. The path will have its ups and downs, but it is best to plan for it to be mostly uphill. The truth is that life revolves around struggle.
2. The path is long, and so you must train for it. Stamina is key.
3. You are wise to pace yourself to ensure you conserve needed energy.
4. Your ability to be creative will help you overcome the many challenges you will face.
5. It is best to take the journey with others as there is power in numbers.

This is where the **Sacred Mission Statement** comes in. It is where you will distill your vision in order to achieve and flow with the aforementioned considerations.

Using the previous chapters as building blocks, start with the vision for where you want to go. Start by being intentional and mindful of your life's purpose. Use your warrior's mindset to set empowering goals. Use what I call the "Circle of Responsibility" to consider what direction you want to travel. We will cover the Circle of Responsibility in the next chapter.

Using the **success paradigm** already discussed in Chapter 6, you can then focus on acquiring the knowledge, attitude, skills, and habits needed for happiness and success. As you continue to learn, grow, share, serve, lead, and inspire, you will be expanding your capacity and with it your potential. You will have learned the leadership core competencies to help you navigate the Master's Path. All this requires you to start with <u>what you will stand for</u>. What you will *live* for.

A Sample Sacred Mission Statement

What follows is an empowering personal mission statement you may borrow.

> *I know that the giving of quality service is my ultimate mission. It is truly my gift to humankind. I accomplish this by striving to be my best self. My goal is to live at a higher level. To achieve this, I focus on being more and doing more. I also help others unlock their fullest potential, mentally, physically, emotionally, and spiritually. I empower others as I empower myself.*
>
> *As part of my purpose, I continue to practice the following essential beliefs:*
>
> – *I treat every person I meet as if they are the most important person in the world because to them they are, because that is the way I want to be treated, and because it is the right thing to do.*
>
> – *I arrange my priorities as if my life depended on them because it does.*

Mastering Strategic Planning and Warrior Tactics

- *I give much more of myself than anyone else could expect of me because they deserve it, so do I, and so does the surrounding community.*
- *I pay close attention to detail, remembering that small things make a huge difference. The little things don't mean a little they mean a lot.*
- *I never compromise with honesty, always asking myself if this is honest and the best I can do.*

And as part of my purpose, I continue to practice these essential beliefs:

I stay focused on my vital tasks and significant goals. I also never forget that the goal is not to finish the list but to enjoy the process and always persist. I know when the student is ready, the teacher will appear. As part of my sacred mission, I ask myself empowering questions every day, such as:

- *What is the most valuable use of my time? This is the WIN principle or <u>What's Important Now</u>?*
- *Why am I here, and what is my primary purpose or sacred mission?*
- *Does this bring me closer or further away from my primary purpose in life?*
- *Am I using my mind as my best friend or my worst enemy?*
- *Do my beliefs still serve me?*

I take this purpose, set definite intelligent plans, and organize the help of others. Specifically, I use my time, energy, and resources to:

– Build confidence & strength in others

- *Inspire hope & mobilize others to act*
- *Connect emotionally with others*
- *Attract & captivate others*

The Ten Step Action Plan for Conquering the Master's Path

To accomplish my sacred mission, I use the following steps to ensure success:

1. I am precise and specific about what I want.
2. I believe without a doubt that my goal is attainable.
3. I know what stands between me and my goals.
4. I study as many aspects of my goal as possible.
5. I obtain the advice of experts and model their beliefs, habits, systems, strategies, and tactics.
6. I create a plan of action based on my studies.
7. I put that plan into action and pilot it if necessary.
8. I adapt, adjust, and revise my plan based on my results.
9. I create a new and improved plan if necessary.
10. Most importantly, I never give up as I know masterpieces are not created overnight.

Carefully consider the keywords used or implied above. They include being <u>precise and specific</u>. That is deciding with specificity in advance.

Belief in yourself is also needed. This comes through believing your goal is attainable. Next is the power of **observation and awareness**. That is, knowing where you are and what you need to learn and *internalize* to move forward successfully. The study

Mastering Strategic Planning and Warrior Tactics

speaks to the necessary **knowledge** to conquer the Master's Path. This is why all great leaders are great readers, by the way. They are not only educated, but they are also *curious.*

Next, the mastermind and modeling power are revealed in number 5. **Creativity** is the key to number 6. It is about creating a plan which requires all the steps before it. Taking **action** is the next step. This is where the rubber meets the road. Nothing happens until you take action. Next, we see where **flexibility** is critical to success. This is important as you will have to **adapt, adjust, and revise** your plan as conditions and your environment change. In number 9, we see where the power of observation and awareness is still in the mix. **Awareness** is key. This is where we employ gap analysis to get back on track and make necessary changes and improvements.

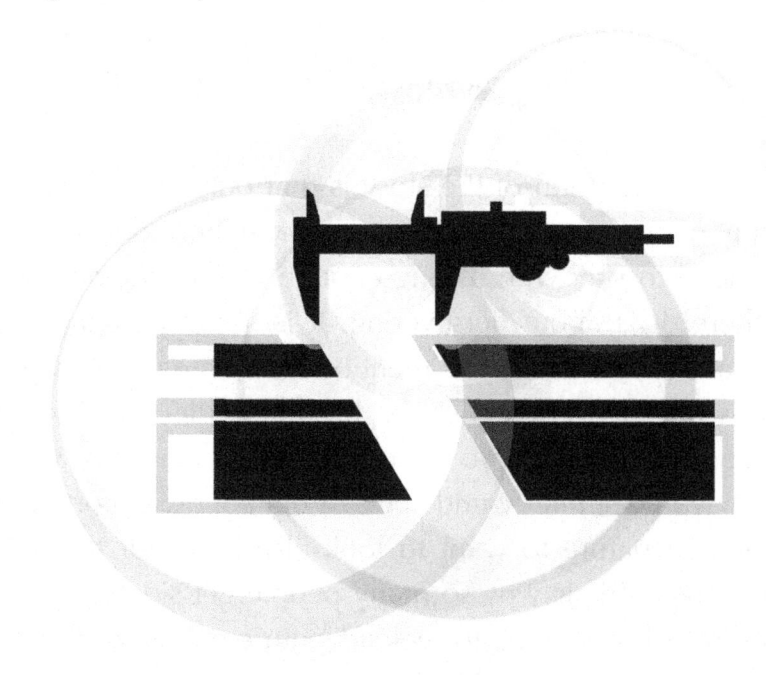

GAP ANALYSIS

Lastly, we come back to the power of **perseverance**. This is where the world-class and the masses often part company. The world-class keep going no matter what comes their way. They don't give up until they arrive at their destination.

Acres of Diamonds

A great book to read on goal attainment is Russell Conwell's classic, *Acres of Diamonds*. The book explores attitudes toward money and wealth. It urges the reader to discover the wealth in front of them rather than search far off places in vain or believe that success is unattainable.

Russell Conwell's story is about an African farmer who is not content with his current life. He decides to sell his property to go off in search of diamonds known to exist in the mines not too far from where he lives. Not long after he sells his farm, the new owner finds acres of diamonds on the same property the farmer had sold.

Of course, the moral of the story is that our most incredible opportunity often exists right where we are, right under our own feet. We need to stay with it long enough to find opportunities already there. It is about persevering. It is about planting your flag and staking your claim. As mentioned in an earlier chapter, the grass is not always greener on the other side. If we would take the time to fully explore the opportunities that exist where we are, we would similarly find acres of diamonds. Unfortunately, it is human nature to want to look elsewhere for the thing we desire most. This is why so many people get sidetracked on their journey. It is one thing to seek adventure and look for other opportunities; it is quite another to be lost, looking for something that already existed under your own two feet.

Before continuing on your journey, I recommend considering that the path you are on may contain exactly what you need most. The ground you stand on may very well hold the joy and happiness you seek. It is important to note that warriors and heroes are *focused,* and as such, they zoom in on where they are. They go deeper to ensure they haven't missed anything important. This includes studying one thing until it is well-rooted. They continually hone their knowledge, attitude, skills, and habits. They look at everything as training. To them, *the journey is the destination.*

Quest Challenge: The Big One

Now that we have looked at what a sacred mission statement might look like, I want you to pause and consider what starts as thought is transformed into reality by action. This requires that you take your dreams and goals and put them on paper. I recommend you use your journal, and yet if you prefer something more high-tech, that's fine. The important thing is that you write it down and look at it often. Remember, whatever you focus on expands. As stated in an earlier chapter, *"Where attention goes, energy flows."*

Take your journal and start with your number one vital task or most important goal. For example: "Launch my coaching website."

> Ask yourself, is this a short-term, mid-term, or long-term goal? Here's what I know, what you can accomplish in five years is impressive. What you hope to achieve in one year is often a pipe dream if your goals are too big. An example is this book. I have been working on this book for years. I am now ready to write it. I have followed the four phases listed below and realized early that the larger the goal, the longer the time frame. However, the good news is that you can break significant goals down into mid-term and short-term objectives or tasks or what I call <u>priority action items</u>.
>
> Now, leave this Quest Challenge exercise aside. We will continue working on it shortly.

Strategic Planning 101 – Getting from Where You Are to Where You Want to Be

Goals are not goals at all if you don't make plans for attaining them – and strategic ones at that. There are four phases to **strategic planning**:

1. Identify Your Strategic Objectives
2. Collect Intel
3. Plan for the Environment
4. Program for Engagement

I now want to share a story with you to give you an idea of how to implement the above process.

In a previous life, I ran a sports and event marketing company called Paragon Promotion Group, Inc. It was small, but we had big dreams. We focused primarily on promoting, marketing, and organizing motorsport events, including festivals and rallies. My

MASTERING STRATEGIC PLANNING AND WARRIOR TACTICS

love of motorcycles (especially Harley's), cars, and music allowed me to use some of my natural abilities to help local businesses and at least several national brands increase their revenue. One example that comes to mind was an event we worked on that took place at the Georgia Dome in the mid-90s. We had been allowed to work with NASCAR and their major sponsor (a national restaurant chain) to provide world-class custom show bikes at the event to celebrate what is now called the NAPA 500. The thought was that the show bikes and custom builders would complement the stock cars, celebrity race car drivers, and The Charlie Daniels band, the headliner musical act.

Up to this point, I had never contemplated taking custom show bikes inside an arena the size of the Georgia Dome. This said, I identified our **strategic objective** and then started to **collect intel**. This included speaking with my partner, an attorney, to figure out the best way to pull it off and minimize risk. After speaking with our clients, we decided to put a few of the very best show bikes on the floor with the stock cars, and then I invited friends and associates with top-end custom Harley's to place their bikes around the terrace level inside the dome. We probably had about 50 custom hot rod bikes on display. I also knew that the kind of show bikes I needed for the arena floor would require motorcycles in the price range of between 50 to $100,000. Motorcycles like this are not easy to come by, so I got busy making phone calls to some of the top motorcycle dealers and custom builders in the southeast. Fortunately, I utilized the **5-step process for attracting and captivating others** reviewed in the previous chapter. That is:

- I found common ground by building rapport.
- I complimented sincerely (I was a good finder).

- I shared my story as opposed to selling something.
- I invited them to join us.
- I planted my flag and staked my claim (I stuck with it)

The truth is at the time I was doing this, I had no idea that I was employing a 5-step process. Building rapport has always come naturally to me. I love people, so striking up a conversation has never been a challenge. This said, when it came to pulling off the details, I was flying by the seat of my pants. The good news I surrounded myself with those who were strong in the areas I was weak. This is known as **the mastermind principle**, which we will cover at the end of this chapter.

As a result of my phone calls, I secured several top builders and their elite show bikes for the arena's floor. One drove up from Daytona, Florida. Another came down from Virginia. One brought his rig down from North Carolina. I had dozens of friends locally who wanted to participate by bringing their custom bikes.

Most importantly, I had a core team of my best friends (my mastermind) who all had their specialties. Glenn is an engineer by training and handled logistics and oversaw security. Sam is an industrial designer and helped me with specialty design and graphics. Larry is an attorney (my partner at the time) and helped me with risk management and contracts. Greg is a renaissance man of sorts and helped me with miscellaneous items. I handled sales and marketing including sponsorships and vendors and oversaw organizing the event, including working with celebrities. I had another friend (more of an acquaintance) who was close friends with the marketing director for a Fortune 500 company and significant national brand. Through this connection, I secured radio spots in the local market at no cost to us. This was a great example of the "ripple effect" in action.

Similarly, I had plenty of close students who were willing to work as security personnel. It is nice to have a large downline of black belt students. In this case, it was easy to find students who loved to attend our events and were more than happy to work the bandstand or stage or fashion show runway. The Georgia Dome also had their security staff, so I felt somewhat confident in our ability to protect the valuable assets present.

This all fell under the category of **planning for the environment**. I knew we needed to safeguard these beautiful race cars, especially the custom show bikes. I was not as concerned about the stock cars as each race team had their people handle that. What I was worried about, however, is that I knew that festival attendees would be enjoying themselves. Some would be enjoying themselves too much. You see, in addition to the race cars, show bikes, and Charlie Daniels, there was that major sponsor who was providing their trademark beverage known by its first three letters "Bud." And, of course, there was the fashion show. I am sure you get the picture.

It was now time to start **programming for engagement**. We had to get all these expensive toys in the Georgia Dome and then make sure everything was set up before the festival. It required a lot of planning but, more importantly, effective communication. Celebrities had to be notified. Sponsors had to be updated and set up booths the day of the event. Entertainment needed to be coordinated. I learned a great deal from putting on the occasion. Most of all, I realized that strategic planning was a master skill that is worth honing and pays valuable dividends.

I also learned how to use warrior tactics from my many years of martial arts training for business success. The good news is you don't have to be a martial arts master to master these skills. They are nothing more than tools and techniques that help you work smarter, not harder.

Warrior Tactics

Warrior tactics are tools to maximize effectiveness. They are used for **acceleration** or **momentum, leverage, multiplication, compounding,** and when needed **to buy time**. As stated earlier, nothing gets done without action. The secret is to avoid spinning your wheels. It is to gain traction when needed most. This is where warrior tactics come in. Imagine them as the specific tools and techniques used to execute plans. They consist of:

- Reading the opponent (knowing your goals)
- Controlling the fighting range (creating space and or buying time)
- The ability to feint effectively (pilot and test before full execution)
- Using proper rhythm and timing (from transition to implementation)
- Escaping, evading, and/or intercepting (i.e., knowing when to hold them and when to fold them so to speak. This includes GAP analysis.)

Reading the opponent simply means goal setting and deciding what you want. This includes reading yourself first and foremost and then knowing your opponent. That is knowing your strengths and weaknesses as well as your opponents. It includes: who, what, when, where, how, and most importantly, why.

Mastering Strategic Planning and Warrior Tactics

What follows is an excellent example of reading your opponent from the outrageous and often bizarre playbook of Sir Richard Branson, founder of the Virgin Group. In this example, Sir Richard took to driving a tank through the streets of New York to promote his new product.

This was a great example of marketing you can't buy. In this case, Branson was promoting his new product Virgin Cola. Even though Virgin Cola ended up falling flat, the grand introduction to the U.S. was explosive — quite literally. Branson took to the streets of New York in a tank, smashing through a wall of coke cans and then appearing to destroy a large Coke sign with the tank's gun. In this case, Coke may have had the high ground when it came to advertising dollars and media exposure, but Virgin Cola seized the day by creating a bang both literally and figuratively.

Controlling the fighting range is understanding the best way to approach the goal, including timeframes such as short-term, mid-term, and or long-term goals. It is the ability to know that the size of the goal determines the amount of time and space you need to accomplish it. It can also include taking the high ground by knowing your environment before execution.

The ability to feint effectively means not telegraphing or projecting your intentions until you are ready. It also means sometimes getting creative in announcing your intentions to maintain the high ground. Once again, from the playbook of billionaire Sir Richard Branson, we see him taking on British Airways (B.A.). Sir Richard used creativity in his battle against B.A. in Virgin Atlantic's early days to include using memorable guerrilla marketing techniques for those of you not familiar with the ability to feint effectively. One example was placing an airship above the

BA-sponsored *"London Eye"* Ferris Wheel when they were having problems erecting the structure. The Virgin airship had a sign on either side emblazoned with, "BA CAN'T GET IT UP!". Talk about throwing your opponent off guard.

The use of proper rhythm and timing is essential in reaching your goals. It is also an understanding that timing is usually the difference between success and failure in any endeavor. It is also an understanding that minor differences over time create significant improvements. This is where the <u>*compound effect*</u> kicks in. Warriors and heroes understand that success is often achieved in inches or small steps, not quantum leaps. They know that even small incremental increases or improvements lead to significant gains over time. This starts with mindset first and then action to follow.

The ability to escape, evade and/or intercept are tactics that every warrior or hero has honed through years of practice. This goes back to creating or closing the gap and sometimes just stepping aside or looking at things from different angles or in different ways. In fighting and goal achievement, the warrior understands the importance of strategic planning and proper tactics.

Over the past 40 years, I have done hundreds of seminars and clinics in my capacity as a master instructor. Later in my career, as the founder of the Atlantic-Pacific Tang Soo Do Federation, I was fortunate to teach subjects as diverse as leadership training and the art of pedagogy, including training for trainers. Whether teaching a mental curriculum or physical technique, I was always interested in using warrior tactics to maximize performance. This

Mastering Strategic Planning and Warrior Tactics

is quickly done with self-defense, free sparring, forms practice, breaking, traditional martial arts weapons, or the healing or soft arts. For example, using the warrior tactics already described, the practitioner of self-defense or sparring can see that reading your opponent has to do with the concept of "partners versus opponents" and sparring whether your partner is an offensive or defensive/counter fighter.

Controlling the fighting range is focused on getting in and getting out quickly or maintaining the high ground. It is about creating space and or closing the gap when and where it is needed most.

Feinting effectively focuses on using your eyes, shoulders, hands, and feet, including switching stances quickly and or using redirection with your hands and feet to disguise intent. It can also be feinting one's ability or skill set, as you will see in the story to follow.

Different timing and rhythm can be seen in sparring using lunges and blitzes, and pattern interrupts such as changing stances quickly and often to confuse your opponent or competitor.

Finally, the tactics of escaping, evading, and/or intercepting can be seen in both self-defense and sparring. If the tactic of intercept is used, those who live the martial way must judiciously use the skills they have learned. Since warriors and heroes are trained against severe attacks, they have an extra responsibility to only use what they have learned the right way. This goes back to thinking a certain way.

Quest Challenge: Plan Your Work – Work Your Plan

I want you to re-open your journal to the page you worked on earlier; where you've jotted down your biggest, most important goal. Have a look at your goal again and take whatever time is necessary to answer the questions below:

- Do you have a bigger vision or goal than the one you noted in your journal? What it is?
- If you have a bigger vision or goal, why didn't you jot it down? What was keeping you back?
- Are you questioning why things have not worked the way you had hoped?
- Are you looking for success and significance? Or is it something else (like approval or acknowledgment)?
- Have you internalized the strategies and tactics of the warrior's way? How can you apply them to this current goal?
- What can you start learning right now that will take you one step closer to achieving this big goal?

I believe every choice you have made has brought you to this chapter. It takes a specific plan to get from where you are to where you want to be. It takes <u>three important assets</u> to succeed. They are:

1. **Knowledge**
2. **Experience/Skill**
3. **A Mentor/Coach**

You can create three columns on your journal page, using each of the above as their respective titles. Now, jot down under each column whatever applies to your big goal. You can note a plus (+) sign for the assets you have, and a minus sign (−) for the things you have yet to acquire in order to fulfill this goal. Another way to do this is by adding green dots or stickers instead of plus signs, and red ones for minus signs.

Refer back to this page every time you acquire a new piece of knowledge, a skill, or a mentor. You can change the symbols that apply or move the dots around. Aim to gather as many pluses or green dots as possible!

It is essential to understand that there is always another level. I call this *"leveling up."* To move from one level to the next, you must consistently increase your knowledge, attitude, skill, and habits. The most powerful practice you can make is a solid connection with a good mentor, coach, teacher, and or guide to help you to the next level.

Here's what I know from taking the journey. It is easy to get sidetracked. I have discovered from many years of walking the Master's Path that balance in life is the Achilles' heel of most world class-performers. I hear this time and again from my coaching clients. The more they want to achieve, the more difficult it is for them to maintain balance in life. This lack of clarity leads to frustration and a feeling of overwhelm. It also leads to cognitive dissonance and emotional imbalance and often strained relationships.

On the one hand, they want to achieve significance, and yet on the other, they feel overwhelmed by all they have taken on. We wish there would be a healthy mix between work, leisure, and family obligations in a perfect world. Of course, life is not perfect, and nor are we. This is why successful leaders, warriors, and heroes plan their work, including the right mix of rest, relaxation, and rejuvenation. This also includes adapting, adjusting, and revising their plan, and re-focusing on opportunities. It requires designing a life that moves you in the right direction with pauses for reflection and renewal. A nice little acronym to remember this is **PARR** or **P**lan, **A**ct, **R**eview, and **R**enew.

Plan your Work – Work your Plan is about designing an action plan for each day, each week, each month, and each year. It's like creating a roadmap to a pre-determined destination with plenty of stops at rest centers, points of interest, and from time to time just to stop and smell the roses.

By taking the time to create a **Massive Action Plan (MAP)** with proper pauses, you'll be joining the ranks of the Top 1% Elite Achievers Club.

The Mastermind – Leveraging Other People's Talents

It's hard to improve when you have no one else's counsel but your own. The **mastermind principle** uses the compound effect related to surrounding yourself with a group of people to acquire advice, counsel, and or for brainstorming. That is, multiplying your knowledge by selecting team members who have expertise in areas where you don't.

THE MASTERMIND

There are two benefits to employing the mastermind principle. One is economical, and the other is psychic or spiritual if you prefer. Sometimes referred to as energetic determination in this book.

There are some essential acronyms to become familiar with related to the mastermind principle. They are:

- **OPK** = Other People's Knowledge
- **OPI** = Other People's Ideas
- **OPS** = Other People's Skills
- **OPE** = Other People's Energy or Equity
- **OPM** = Other People's Money

When we speak about OPK or OPI, there are many ways to acquire it. The quickest and easiest is via the internet. Another is found in any well-stocked public library. A third way and probably the best way is to create your group of select team members who specialize or have expertise in various fields of study you do not. For example, Henry Ford, the founder of the Ford Motor Company, overcame poverty, illiteracy, and ignorance to create one of the most successful companies in the world by surrounding himself with some of the brightest minds of his time. Through his association with Thomas Edison and other significant business and scientific greats, Henry Ford could tap into the knowledge and ideas of the best minds around. The same can be said of Andrew Carnegie, the great steel magnate and founder of the Carnegie Steel Company, which became U.S. Steel Corporation. Carnegie's mastermind group consisted of a group of approximately fifty team members.

When we speak about OPS and OPE, Mahatma Gandhi is a great example that comes to mind. His example, much like that of Martin Luther King, demonstrates the more psychic and or spiritual side of the mastermind. In Gandhi's case, this somewhat eccentric figure was able to garner great power by coordinating over two hundred million people. He was able to tap into the energetic determination and spirit of harmony of the masses for a definite purpose. In this case, to gain India's freedom from their British overlords. To accomplish this, it took OPS and OPE, and it took the relentless drive, desire, faith, persistence, and of course, action.

We know from studying and employing the mastermind that when someone can effectively use the principle, they can acquire

Mastering Strategic Planning and Warrior Tactics

and utilize OPK, OPI, OPS, OPE, and obtain OPM or other people's money. This is one of the bedrock principles of capitalism. Every great venture capitalist has to harness OPK, OPI, OPS, and OPE to gain OPM. This is how wealth is accumulated.

It requires a superior thinking process where one uses strategic planning, warrior tactics, and the mastermind principle to leverage or level up.

As we finish this chapter, just keep in mind that two good minds are better than one. Truthfully, no two minds ever come together without effectively creating a third mind. In this case, the coming together of great minds compounds. Similarly, three good minds become four, and so on. This is why heroes prefer to team up. They realize that by leveraging other people's knowledge, ideas, skills, talents, energy, equity, and money, along with their own, they are better positioned to create win/win/win situations. That is situations or opportunities that are good for them, good for their team members, and good for the community. When done correctly, the mastermind principle can make a significant positive impact in your life.

Quest Challenge: Create Your Mastermind

Answer the following questions to create your mastermind:
- What do I need to read?
- Who do I need to call?
- Who do I need to invite into my inner circle?
- What do I need to do to create a lasting legacy?

As continue along the Master's Path, we will focus in Chapter 8 on being the example through understanding and using **the Circle of Responsibility**.

Chapter 8

Mastering the Circle of Responsibility

"Success is not for those who want it, nor those who need it, but for those who are utterly determined to seize it – whatever it takes." – Darren Hardy

Are you ready for the next level of challenge? If so, congratulations; you are well on your way! And you are more prepared than ever to continue your journey along the Master's Path.

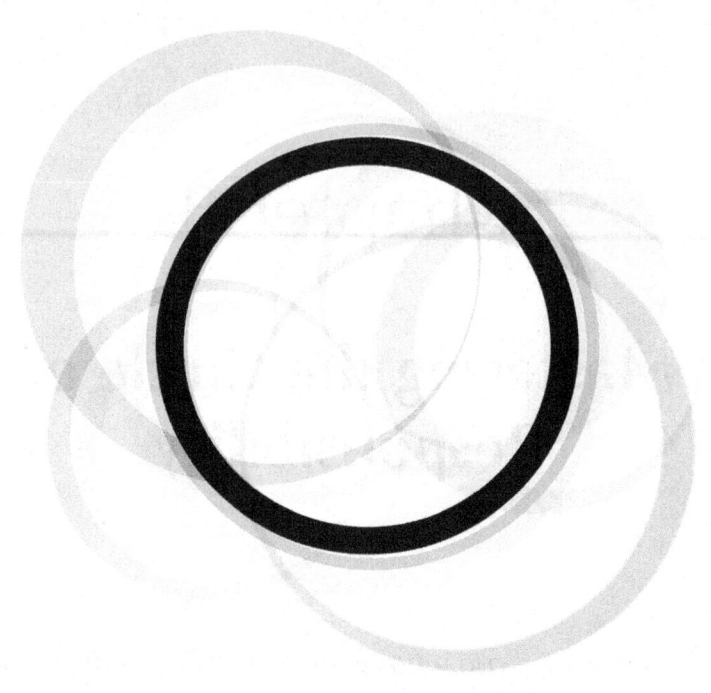

THE CIRCLE OF RESPONSIBILITY

This chapter will explore what I call the **Circle of Responsibility**. But what does that even mean?

The hero, warrior, and champion understand that they must master themselves first and foremost. Self-control is imperative. So is discipline. The word *responsibility* can be broken into two smaller words, *response* and *ability*. It applies to everything you do. Remember the words, "I am responsible". Or the phrase, "If it is to be, it is up to me," made famous by Zig Ziglar and others.

So, what precisely is the circle of responsibility? Imagine in your mind's eye a wheel with many spokes. The middle of the wheel is a hub to keep the spokes in alignment and place. Imagine the intersection at the center is beautifully chromed with the words "I am responsible" engraved on it.

Next, imagine that each spoke is the same length to ensure proper balance. Each spoke in this wheel represents your life. For example, if we zoom out, the spokes represent your general attitude and mindset, relationships (family/friends), job, career, or better yet, you're calling. It also includes your community (including charitable pursuits), your health & fitness, spiritual life, finances, and education, including your vocation and hobbies. These areas of responsibility are seen through the lens of the Master's Path, with a particular focus on heightened <u>awareness</u>, <u>focus</u>, and <u>balance</u>.

The hero understands that their journey is ultimately their responsibility and no one else's. In a previous chapter, we discussed the **STAR** acronym or principle, *Success Through Accepting Responsibility.*

If we were to change the context of the circle of responsibility for a moment, we could zoom in on any of these life spokes and focus on a different set of training concepts and principles. Take, for example, traditional martial arts. The spokes could represent character and leadership traits, the history, tradition, culture, philosophy, and the physical skills of forms practice, self-defense, weapons, sparring, breaking, teaching, and overall fitness.

Suppose we changed the context of the wheel to zoom in on overall fitness. In that case, the spokes could represent conditioning, endurance and or stamina, flexibility, speed control, strength or power control, balance/agility, timing/rhythm, and mental attitude.

It is important to note that all the spokes have to be of equal length and equally strong for the wheel to roll smoothly. They also have to be in balance and alignment. If anyone is out of balance, other areas of responsibility will suffer. For example, if we focus too much on career or calling, our relationships with family and friends will suffer. Similarly, if we focus too much on finances, we may find our health and fitness adversely affected.

If the goal is to enjoy life and be happy, we must remain balanced or centered. In this case, to have peace and calm, we are wise to master the circle of responsibility.

The Way of the Dragon

In his book, the Secret Power Within, Chuck Norris gives the example of Bruce Lee. He mentions a visit to Bruce Lee's home and how impressed he was with Bruce Lee's library, which included books on various subjects, from Zen, the Laws of Physics, popular books on child-raising, and a myriad of books on philosophies of the world. He also had many books on martial arts, boxing, fitness, and topics as diverse as ballet, dancing, and nutrition.

In his short but accomplished life, Bruce Lee indelibly etched his persona on Hollywood history, popular culture, and the hearts of martial arts fans everywhere. He helped introduce martial arts to the modern world with his Jeet Kune Do's style (The Way of the Intercepting fist). He also starred in and helped produce five mainstream films that influenced popular culture worldwide. But few knew the man behind the lightning-fast moves. He truly embodied the way of the dragon.

He was nothing short of a phenomenon. As an example, in his short time on this planet, he accomplished the following:

- He was one of the first Asian action movie heroes.
- He kicked down racial barriers – literally.

- He opened the martial arts to the masses.
- He pioneered free running.
- He was an early pioneer of the self-help movement.
- He invented creative ways to develop strength, power, and speed, including innovative training equipment and devices.
- He helped develop the nutritional shake market with his high protein mix.
- He shaped superhero culture.
- He co-starred as Kato in the Green Hornet and became one of the first well-known Asian TV stars.
- He was an author, philosopher-king, and mentored some of the best-known movie stars of his day at his school and his home.

Bruce Lee was also very human. He had difficulties being accepted when he first started his career. To many in the traditional martial world, he was a threat. This was particularly true of those who studied traditional Kung Fu. He also suffered due to his unrelenting focus on his career. His marriage suffered, and so did other vital relationships.

Ultimately, Bruce Lee was a massive success in many ways, yet he died too young. One can only imagine what he would have accomplished if he was still living.

It is easy to lose sight of what matters most when we have too many irons in the fire. The Master's Path is not only long; it requires focus on what is most important. The way or journey is full of struggle, as we mentioned earlier. It is also full of growth opportunities. It is essential to keep your sacred mission or purpose in mind while on the hero's journey. Finding balance is vital. This requires awareness and the ability to know when to say no.

Time for Clarity

While I am no Bruce Lee, I have experienced firsthand how life can become unbalanced when we lose sight of what is most important. There are too many examples to share in this chapter but suffice to say that the late '80s in Bloomington, Illinois was one of them. As you know from a previous chapter, I was employed by State Farm Insurance as a training analyst at their corporate headquarters. I was in my late 20s and felt the world was my oyster. I had opened an at-risk martial arts program for disadvantaged children and adults at a local community center. I was able to gain the support of my company as they realized I had a passion for helping kids and adults in trouble. I also had my martial arts school called United Karate Academy, which met in our basement two times per week. At this time, I was also serving on the Board of Directors of an international martial arts organization as finance and business director. If this wasn't enough, I served as the regional coordinator in the Midwest and assisted the Grandmaster with helping to recruit new schools. Somewhere in there, I decided I wanted to start a martial arts business publication called Business Master.

I convinced a dear friend at State Farm to partner with me in the venture. Although my friend was not in martial arts, he was very talented and knew technology well. As it turned out, Business Master was one of the very first martial arts business publications offered in the United States by subscription. Things were rolling along well when my friend decided he would like me to join the local branch of the Freemasons. He was a high-ranking member of the local Blue Lodge. I must admit, I was intrigued with the thought of joining the masons, which had members as famous as 14 presidents of the United States, 35 United States supreme court justices, 17 United States senators, 32 United States military leaders, and 13 signers of the U.S. constitution.

What can I say? I was young and had visions of greatness. Let's face it, if the Freemasons were good enough for George Washington, Benjamin Franklin, John Hancock, Paul Revere, Theodore Roosevelt, Franklin Delano Roosevelt, and Samuel Clemens (aka Mark Twain), to name a few; it might be just good enough for me. This reminds me of something one of my mentors once shared with me. He said, "When you are young, you have a lot of energy but not much wisdom. When you are old, you have more wisdom but less energy." He said, "This is why you must work smarter, not harder, as you mature and gain age." At this time in my journey, I had no shortage of energy and ambition. Of course, as the old Chinese maxim goes, "In the valley of the blind, one eye is king." My short-sightedness was my focus on titles, ranks, and positions.

Hindsight is 20/20. After earning a 3rd degree Master Mason's rank in the Freemason's Scottish Rite Blue Lodge that same year, I decided to see how many more plates I could spin. I had just tested for a 3rd-degree black belt in Tang Soo Do the year before. Up to this point, I had only competed in tournaments in the Northeast, California, and Mexico. I wanted to see how I stacked up against practitioners of different styles and organizations in the Midwest, so I started traveling in the Midwest to compete on the open martial arts tournament circuit with my students. I won a couple of grand championship titles along the way despite the chaos of open tournaments at that time. After seeing how poorly tournaments were organized, I decided to host my first open tournament that same year with the Grandmaster's permission. With the help of another friend, I also decided to create a start-up called Professional Karate Tournaments of America. It was to be a tournament league, or at least that was what I had envisioned.

It was about this same time that I received a call from the President of the martial arts organization I belonged to asking me how things were going. He knew I was busy and checked in on me, which I appreciated. When I asked him how he was, he expressed frustration with how slow progress was with his first book, entitled Traditional Tang Soo Do, Volume 1, The Essence. I asked him how I could help. He shared how he was stuck trying to put his notes in a format that would make sense to future readers. At this point, I offered to help him over the hump. He later wrote on the acknowledgments page, "Jeff St. James prodded me into assembling my notes into a tangible manuscript, and his wife, Mercy, was gracious enough to pose for the photos in the exercise chapter of this book."

The backstory was I invited the Grandmaster to spend a week with us at our home in Bloomington, and I took off work to help him compile his notes. I will never forget him opening up a small suitcase in our dining room while pulling out his handwritten notes, complete with paste-up diagrams and, in some cases, stick-figure sketches he had made. It took the better part of the day to put them in some semblance of order, but I could see he was passionate about getting it done, and I was honored to be of service. As he shared his thoughts, concepts, and desires, I tried to keep up taking notes in my composition book. It soon became apparent that I would need to think more intelligently rather than work harder. I then asked the Grandmaster if he would be okay with me using a micro-recorder to record his thoughts, and I would then take everything and help organize it. I made my notes of significant points on index cards from the micro-recorder. I then helped organize the manuscript, which would become the eventual first book. When writing the original manuscript for the instructor training manual, I used the same system, which would become his fifth book. I later used the same method to write the Atlantic-Pacific Tang Soo Do Federation's Certified Instructor Training Program and accompanying manuals. I have often used this same system to help build businesses both large and small. I learned from this experience that you can more easily duplicate success once you have the right systems, strategies, and procedures in place.

"Champions are Masters of Mental Organization"
– Steve Seibold

The Grandmaster and I spent the better part of a week working on the project. My karate students were honored to have the Grandmaster join us in the basement for a class one evening, and I was thrilled to have time with him every evening to pick his brain. I felt like Daniel-san with Mr. Miyagi as he told me old tales of training with some of the early luminaries from Tang Soo Do history. One was the legendary Chuck Norris himself. I remember asking the Grandmaster what Chuck Norris was like as a student while in Osan, Korea. He told me that Chuck was far from his most talented student. He spoke about him getting "beat up" in many classes by his seniors. He then said to me, "He was never the most talented but was always the hardest working. He came early and stayed late. He took notes on what he learned after each class." He spoke of his earliest experiences teaching "Carlos Norris" and some of the other students he trained at the Osan U.S. Airbase.

Our week together went by very fast, and I looked forward to our time together every evening with our fireside chats. He later wrote me, "Thanks for your motivation and driving power to push this goal. We made it now, and I deeply appreciate your support and care."

The truth is he helped me more than he could ever know. I was so busy being ambitious that I had forgotten why I was training in the first place. It was to become better and develop my potential to serve my students better. I realized that I was dropping plates. The wheel was spinning, but it was not in alignment. I had to focus on organizing my life the same way I was helping the Grandmaster to organize his book. It was time to ask better questions and then learn from them. It was time to focus on what was most important, including preparing for the next leg of the journey. I discontinued my tournament traveling, eventually gave away most of my trophies, gave up Business Master, and said goodbye to the tournament league idea. They were taking too much time, energy, and resources. It was time to go deeper into what was most important. It was time for clarity.

"Excellent performance starts with excellent preparation."
– John St. James

Quest Challenge: Your Circle of Responsibility List

To find peace and happiness, it is wise to follow your purpose and passion while maintaining balance in all areas of your life. This is your circle of responsibility. Do this by creating a list or even sketching "passion bubbles". In each list or bubble, note the passion at the very top, and at least five responsibilities associated with it below or within the bubble.

For example:

Passion: Skiing in the Alps

Responsibilities

1) Equipment purchase and maintenance
2) Holiday arrangements 6 months in advance
3) Sort out all pending work/tasks/deadlines prior to allocating time off
4) Skiing lessons or practice on a smaller range
5) Spend equal time with family (if not taking them with me)

Once you create your circle of responsibility list, determine your overall purpose and make sure your list reinforces it. What is the one responsibility you have which will give your life the most meaning? Lastly, review your daily goals and remember not to become a prisoner of your desires.

In the next chapter, we will move on to how to best **serve others while living an empowered life**.

PHASE 3
Leading and Inspiring

Chapter 9

Living an Empowering Life While Being a Catalyst for Positive Change

Congratulations! You have made it to Phase 3 of *The Master's Path*. As you know from previous chapters, the success paradigm consists of three phases. This phase is all about **leading and inspiring**.

Of course, this assumes you are leading someone. As an old mentor of mine once said, "If you are a leader with no followers, you are not leading. The good news, however, is that we *all* lead someone. Some of you are teaching yourself and hence in a leadership role. Others are leading family members or children, and some of you are leading students as school owners. Some of you are business owners and lead a group of team members or employees. Many of you are leading co-workers as part of your full-time career. Whatever your specific situation, you will discover in this chapter that your mission is to lead by the habit of giving your best effort and reaching your full potential. By doing this, you will be living an empowering life while being a catalyst for positive change in the lives of others. You will also be making a positive change in your own life.

Making an Extraordinary Effort

Whether we are talking about work, school, or business, you will always succeed at a higher level if you develop the habit of giving your best effort as you serve others.

Nobody achieves greatness by being lazy or giving a half-hearted effort. If you have any doubt, all you have to do is look at the best in any field. Whether it is Sir Richard Branson, Jeff Bezos, or other top business leaders, you will see that they continue to lead and inspire as part of their daily existence. It is that special extra effort that turns the ordinary into the extraordinary.

If you study champions' training in any sport or business, you will see them putting in hours of dedicated practice and giving their best effort to get better. You will also see them serving at a higher level. The same holds for warriors and heroes along the Master's Path.

When you give your best effort and consistently push to exceed your previous best, you will get better, and you will improve. With time and training, you will excel. With time, people will look at you as the exception. You will indeed be exceptional.

Never allow minimums to become your maximums. Always strive to be better!

The **Law of Incremental Improvement** proves this. When you push yourself to your current best and then strive for 10%

improvement or better, you will constantly raise the bar on your personal best. Even minor improvements over time add up. The compound effect kicks in, and before long, you are achieving truly terrific things. Your ability to lead and inspire affects your ability to make a positive impact in the lives of others. You become more valuable over time because you add more value to people.

The difference between ordinary and extraordinary is one word: extra!

You will take yourself to new levels of excellence if you decide in advance to give extra effort and *exceptional* service. The opposite is also true. If you get in the habit of providing a minimal effort and accept less than your best, this can also become a habit. Remember, *habits we train are habits we gain.*

So, what can you do to pick up the pace to improve your skills? What could you do to exceed expected and provide extraordinary service? What could you do in your relationships to make a profound and positive impact on those around you? How can you lead at a higher level?

At work, can you arrive a little earlier, stay later, improve your effort and increase your overall contribution? At home, could you help more with chores and or take the initiative to improve things? What else could you do?

The Law of Empowerment

When it comes to empowering others, the **Law of Empowerment** states that only secure leaders give power to others. The best leaders are willing to share leadership duties. Stated differently, confident leaders do not have to be in charge. They can still maintain control and at the same time empower those around them to learn, grow, share, serve, lead, and inspire.

I have found over time that to be a good leader; you have to make mistakes and learn from those mistakes. Similarly, by empowering your team, you are giving them the ability to create and learn from their mistakes.

Here are some **essential considerations for empowering others:**

- ✓ Believe in yourself
- ✓ Believe in those you empower
- ✓ Make empowering others your focus
- ✓ Remember, leading well is not about enriching yourself; it's about improving others.
- ✓ You can only have more if you contribute more. Focus on being <u>value-added</u>.
- ✓ Delegating is different than abdicating. Be available to help whenever needed.
- ✓ It is not what you get but rather what you become. Become more.
- ✓ You can only do so much on your own. Be a master team builder.
- ✓ By empowering others, you find the talents of others will multiply your efforts and more quickly lead to victory for all.

Barriers to Empowerment

The number one barrier to empowerment is the desire to be in control. In the workplace, it often boils down to job security.

Take, for example, the boss or leader afraid a co-worker, team member, or subordinate will take their job if they put them in charge. Rather than using a growth mindset, the inexperienced leader is afraid they will lose control if they give too much responsibility to someone else. The fear of loss is more potent in most people than the opportunity for growth.

Another barrier to empowerment is resistance to change. Most people are afraid of change. They live for the status quo, too scared to step out of their comfort zones. The truth is that the only way to grow is to change. Change is the price of progress. When I was a young man, I remember my father telling me, "The one thing in life that is constant is change."

The Climb

To live an empowering life while being a positive catalyst for change, you must focus on the success paradigm and the success cycle. I often tell my leadership students and clients that the Master's Path is much like climbing a mountain. It takes both the right strategy and the right tactics.

Consider the following:

- ✓ You will need different ideas and strategies at various places in your journey and development. In other words, thinking out of the box has to be ongoing. Your perspective will change with time.
- ✓ You risk the most when you become complacent. You can never rest on your laurels. As circumstances change, you must change to meet new challenges.

- ✓ Your perspective determines your potential. That is, how you see things will determine what you see. I am sure you have heard the old saying, "Keep your eyes on the prize."
- ✓ The good news is it's never been easier to go from zero to massive success. The opposite is true as well. Old school thinking in the 21st Century can quickly lead to obsolescence.
- ✓ Good is not good enough anymore. In the past, good meant you were competitive. Great equaled sure success. Today, good equals dead. The excellent survive. The greats thrive and flourish.
- ✓ What gets measured gets improved. You must not only track what you do but actively work towards improving weak areas.

How many of you remember Blockbuster Video? I can still remember going to Blockbuster to look for a handful of movies I wanted to watch. Of course, this required getting in the car and driving down to the local Blockbuster store. It also required waiting in line to checkout and then going home after a quick stop at the store to pick up snacks. Sure, you could get popcorn at the Blockbuster and candy, but the choices were limited. Also, when it came time to return the video rentals if you were like most people, you had held on to them too long and had incurred late fees. Blockbuster's business model was counting on that. I was once told by a Blockbuster employee that they made more money off of late fees than they did from renting the movies. There is an important lesson here. Procrastination can lead to failure or temporary gain—depending on how it is used.

Unfortunately for Blockbuster, they failed to see the future. Netflix saw the future, and they are flourishing. Old business models and old school thinking become dinosaurs faster today than at any time in history. This is why if you want to live an empowering life and be a positive catalyst for change, you need to plan ahead and be willing to change.

I had mentioned that the Master's Path was like climbing a mountain. As mentioned in a previous chapter, everything that is worthwhile is uphill, including the summit. If you want to be a summit seeker, your strategy and tactics at base camp will differ from camp 2 or 20,000 feet. Similarly, your approach at camp 3 or 30,000 feet will need to be evaluated and changed once again.

Fortunately, the Master's Path is not only uphill; it has its shares of plateaus. It also has crevices and cliffs. Blockbuster may have made it to camp three but found a cliff before reaching the summit.

To ensure you don't find a cliff, you need to understand the power of plateaus. A plateau is not only a great place to rest; it is a great place to reflect on where you have been and what you need to get to the next level. If we continue the mountain climbing metaphor, it is at the plateau where you set up a temporary camp to check your plan and make sure it still makes sense. For the mountain climber, this is where they check their equipment, the weather forecast, and take stock of necessary supplies. It is also where they take stock of themselves to make sure they have the right mindset to continue climbing.

I call this ***stepping up to level up***. You see, too many people stop at a plateau but fail to recognize the opportunity they provide. I see this frequently with clients who say something like,

"Oh, I already know that." Naturally, we all know that knowing something and doing it are two different things. I have heard this referred to as the *disease of knowledge*. People tend to confuse a general knowledge of something with really knowing it. To really know a thing, you have to do it over and over again. To become a master at it requires a very deep dive over an extended time. Let's go back to the mountain climbing metaphor. There is no shortage of people who intellectually understand how to climb a mountain but very few who have summited Mount Everest relative to the total world population. Of course, there are many reasons for this; time, energy, and resources are just a few. Add to this mindset, desire, and preparation, and you start to understand why summiting the great mountain is such a coveted prize. Most people don't see the team it requires to climb a great mountain or achieve anything of great importance. This chapter's focus is on this essential key to success. I hope that if you are reading this, you have the time, energy, and resources to take the challenge. What you may lack is the desire and the team to make it happen.

Planning Ahead While Facing Fear

Building an excellent team is no easy feat. It requires the ability to lead and inspire at a level very few people attain. Here's what I know, your leadership team will help you plan if you have picked your leadership properly and trained them on what is needed to succeed. You might be familiar with the acronym **PLAN AHEAD**. If not, there is a quick review below.

> **P** = Pre-determine the changes needed.
>
> **L** = Lay out the steps in the correct order of implementation.
>
> **A** = Adjust the priorities as necessary.
>
> **N** = Notify key team players.
>
> **A** = Allow time for acceptance.
>
> **H** = Head into action with proper timeframes in place.
>
> **E** = Expect challenges and have contingencies in place to handle them.
>
> **A** = Always point to the success already achieved and stay positive.
>
> **D** = Daily improvement is the key to success.

On your journey along the Master's Path, you will face no shortage of foes. Some of these will be other people, but mostly they will be the enemy within. One such foe is **fear**. As mentioned in an earlier chapter, this includes:

- The fear of the unknown
- The fear of failure
- The fear of loss (including money)
- The fear of certainty (including control)
- The fear of rejection
- The fear of embarrassment
- For some, it is the fear of fear. The pain of failure is so intense that the person never tries.

Quest Challenge: Planning Ahead

Revisit your big goal and re-write it at the top of your journal page. Then, based on the PLAN AHEAD acronym, utilize only the PLAN steps and note down the four actions necessary for implementing your big goal-related plan. In other words:

1. What current changes are needed for this goal to succeed?
2. What steps are required for its implementation?
3. Out of the previous steps, which are the priorities that must be tackled first?
4. Who are your key team players in making this goal a reality?

In the next chapter, we will focus on more than just serving others, but what you can do to truly **raise up and inspire** them.

Chapter 10

The Power to Raise People Up

"There are three kinds of people in the world. There are the well-poisoners who discourage others, stomp on their creativity, and tell them what they can't do. There are the lawnmowers, people who have good intentions but are self-absorbed, who mow their own lawn but never help others. And there are life-enhancers. This last category contains people who reach out to enrich the lives of others, who lift them up and inspire them."
– Walt Disney

I am a big believer in learning how people operate, including understanding people's wants, needs, and desires. Understanding others' motives is an integral part of the process.

And here is one thing I know for sure. Most if not all people want, need, and desire:

- To be heard

- To be seen
- To be empathized with
- To be recognized
- To be cared for
- To be respected
- To be treated as important
- To be liked
- To be loved
- To have structure, consistency, and certainty

Here is what else I know: People want to be guided by someone who cares. That is someone who is dedicated to helping them to the next level and beyond.

This is where you come in. I genuinely believe you were born and are here to help inspire others to live a more empowered life. In this section, we will look at some important considerations to help you do just this.

A "RAE" of Sunshine

RAE stands for:

RECOGNIZE – ACKNOWLEDGE – ENCOURAGE

Praise and recognition are two of the most powerful motivating forces in the world. The truth is people will work harder for praise than a raise. Every one of us loves to be praised and recognized for our efforts. It is truly the heartbeat of human motivation.

I stated above that people need to be liked. The fact is the number one human need is to be <u>validated</u>. That is to be valued. We not only want acceptance; we also get a hit of endorphins

The Power to Raise People Up

when we are. It makes us feel liked and cared for as individuals. If you don't believe me, look at the number of people addicted to getting more "likes" on Facebook.

In an earlier chapter, I mentioned that leadership is the ability to influence others. If you want to lead and inspire others, go from seeking praise to heaping praise. Look for opportunities to heap praise on others for a job well done.

"It is amazing what can be accomplished if you do not care who gets the credit." – Harry Truman

The number one reason why people leave companies is they didn't feel appreciated. Think about that for just a moment. Every one of us has an imaginary sign hanging around our neck that says, "I need love. I need to be valued and appreciated. I need some occasional praise and recognition."

"I've talked to nearly 30,000 people on this show, and all 30,000 had one thing in common. They all wanted validation."
– Oprah Winfrey

It is essential to our survival that we feel understood. We want to be understood and want to be seen, heard, accepted, and approved of. We want our leaders to listen to us and honestly care about how we feel. It goes back to our hard wiring. Our primitive psyche was predicated on "fitting in." A member of the tribe needed to be accepted by the leader. Survival depended on it as far back as when our ancestors hunted and gathered for daily existence. If a member wasn't met with approval, that person no longer felt protected and secure. That hard wiring is seen today in how a political leader can so easily influence the thoughts and behaviors of those in their base. The base is just another way of saying the tribe.

It is essential to understand the need for acceptance, approval, and validation as they are the stepping stones to influence. Here again, if you don't believe me think back to your teenage years. You will no doubt remember trying to fit in with the "in" crowd or perhaps the "anti-crowd," depending on your personality. Either way, you naturally were inclined to associate with others like you. The keyword in the previous sentence is *like*. Those like you were more apt to like you. You were less likely to be rejected by those like you. Our need for acceptance, approval, and validation was and continues to be necessary. We needed the tribe to survive. We needed to "fit" in and be accepted.

When giving praise, there are certain dos to keep in mind. They are:

1. **Be specific** – avoid saying "good job" as it is not clear enough.
2. **Be timely** – give praise when positive behavior happens. Think of providing recognition like providing a tip. It is most appreciated right after the service.
3. **Be unique** – create awards for special attributes like most positive, most timely, most creative, most caring, most spirited.
4. **Be balanced** – too much loses its power. Praise is like seasoning, just enough enhances the flavor and taste, but too much is sickening. Also, remember to praise exceptional, not expected.
5. **Praise publicly** – Put a spotlight on the behavior you want to be repeated. Once you spotlight and highlight what you want, the person will want to do more of what earned them the praise they received.

6. Systemize praise – make it part of your daily, weekly, monthly, and yearly operations.

EQ+ = Exceptional Emotional Intelligence

As a leader, you are in the people business first and foremost. As I stated in an earlier chapter, we like to think we are rational beings who occasionally show emotion. As you now know, we are, in fact, emotional beings who are sometimes rational. Emotional intelligence trumps capability. I am sure you have heard the old statement, "people don't care how much you know as much as they care how much you care."

Top Ten Ways to Raise People Up

The truth is if you want to influence those around you, you need to focus on **emotional engagement**. You need to be committed to becoming:

1. A person who nurtures other people
2. A person who has faith in other people
3. A person who listens to other people
4. A person who understands other people
5. A person who recognizes other people
6. A person who acknowledges other people
7. A person who encourages other people
8. A person who builds up other people
9. A person who navigates for other people
10. A person who empowers others

But it all starts with making the definitive decision to work on your own growth and accelerate it exponentially. Otherwise, how will you raise people and encourage them to see the value in your contribution?

If you want to accelerate your growth and empower more people, you need to start with addition or, better yet, **multiplication**. The more people you add value to, the more your tribe will grow. Using the compound effect, it will eventually multiply exponentially. Think of it this way. First, you need to multiply, then mentor, and then motivate, including <u>nurture</u>.

People must be cared for, not just physically but also emotionally. At the heart of all nurturing is a genuine concern for others. Remember this; people are influenced the most by those that make them feel the best about themselves. Reread this; your job, if you want to empower others, and be a catalyst for positive change, is to help people feel good about themselves. If you can do this mentally, physically, emotionally, and spiritually, you are well on your along the Master's Path.

But nurturing starts with *you*.

I have a question for you. What are you doing to grow yourself and be more of a nurturer, both to yourself and to others? What are you doing to be more of a giver than a getter? How are you adding value to others?

Quest Challenge: Adding Value to Others

What can you do today to add value to others? Use the list below today and this week to help you focus on <u>giving for greatness</u>.

- ✓ Instead of trying to put others in their place, try putting yourself in place.

- ✓ Recognize someone today for a job well done. Remember, be specific and clear.
- ✓ Find someone to acknowledge and at the same time help them feel like they belong.
- ✓ Help someone change their perspective from negative to positive. Remember, it is not who you are that holds you back but rather who you think you are. Again, your perspective determines your potential.
- ✓ Look for someone to encourage. Let them know how important they are as members of your team.
- ✓ Help someone find hope amid a crisis.

I genuinely believe you are capable of this. To further help you, review the list below on how to become a natural nurturer. To get the most out of these tips, focus on cultivating a positive attitude and not just open-mindedness but, more importantly, <u>other</u>-mindedness.

- ✓ Commit to helping others learn
- ✓ Commit to helping others grow
- ✓ Commit to helping others share
- ✓ Commit to assisting others to serve
- ✓ Commit to helping others to become leaders
- ✓ Commit to helping others to inspire others
- ✓ Commit to the Master's Path
- ✓ Commit to giving others opportunities
- ✓ Commit with no strings attached

Facts About Faith in People

Faith in people is an essential quality of leadership. If you want to influence others positively, you need to have faith in them. Here is what I have learned in the past 40 years of developing leaders:

- ✓ Most people don't have faith in themselves
- ✓ Most people don't have someone who has faith in them
- ✓ Most people can tell when someone has faith in them
- ✓ Most people will do anything to live up to your faith in them

As you consider the above, remember, faith is more than thinking something is true. Faith is thinking something is valid to the extent that you act on it. With this in mind, use the list below to become a believer in people:

1. Believe in them before they succeed.
2. Emphasize their strengths and praise them for what they do well both privately and publicly.
3. Instill confidence when they fail. Remember, failure is just an opportunity to learn, grow, and share. Your job is to show them that success is a journey, a process, not a destination, and failure is the price of future success.
4. Experience some wins together. Remember, together, everyone achieves more. (TEAM).
5. Help them find their strengths and focus on those first.
6. Help them find their weaknesses and overcome them.
7. Build on past successes. Remember, the "Power of MO" or momentum.

8. Start right. Help team members build some quick and easy wins.

Moving From Maintenance to Multiplication – A Person of Influence Empowers People

Unfortunately, most people live in maintenance mode. Rather than focus on making progress, they prefer to keep from losing ground. I have found that it is better to mentor your team members, so they see the power of multiplication.

When you hear the word empower, what comes to mind? For many, it is simple mathematics. For me, it is the source code of leadership and conjures up what it means to empower others. Consider planting seeds today for a fruitful harvest in the future. I want you also to consider the following:

- When you empower people, you're not influencing just them; you're influencing all the people they influence.
- When you become a person who empowers, you work with and through people.
- The act of empowering people is a win-win situation for you and the people you are empowering.
- You have not lost anything by empowering others but instead multiplied your influence.

There are specific qualifications needed to be a person who empowers. Consider the pre-requisites. Without the following qualifications, you will find the path full of obstacles:

- Position – It is impossible to empower those you do not lead.
- Relationship – Real relationships are forged, not formed.

- Respect – Relationships may cause people to want to be with you, but respect causes them to want to be empowered by you.
- Commitment – How dedicated are you to the process? Is there anything that would keep you from completing your calling? If so, I recommend you are honest with yourself and others about it.

Quest Challenge: Looking Inward Before Empowering Others

Take the time to answer the following questions before you get started empowering others:

- Do I believe in people and feel that they are my organization's most appreciable asset?
- Do I believe that empowering others can accomplish more than individual achievement?
- Do I actively search for potential leaders to empower?
- Would I be willing to raise others to a level higher than my level of leadership?
- Would I be willing to invest time, energy, and resources in developing people who have leadership potential?
- Would I be willing to let others get credit for what I taught them?
- Do I allow others freedom of personality and process, or do I have to be in control?
- Would I be willing to give my authority and influence to potential leaders publicly?

The Power to Raise People Up

- Would I be willing to let others work me out of a job?
- Would I be willing to hand the leadership baton to the people I empower and genuinely root for them to succeed?

If you answered no to more than a couple of these questions, you might be like most other people. Unfortunately, the human condition is difficult to overcome at times. Don't worry; you are on the Master's Path, which means that the teacher will appear when the student is ready.

I look forward to helping you on your heroic journey along the Master's Path. You are well on your way. The key is to stick with it.

Chapter 11

Living Honorably

Do you want to be a person of integrity and live an honorable life? If you've answered affirmatively, then you'll be glad to know that this is what this chapter is all about.

In this chapter, you will learn the supreme attribute of the hero, the warrior, and the champion. If you thoroughly learn and act upon this attribute, you will be passing life's most significant character tests. To do this, you must become pure of heart, honor, and integrity. You must also show courage which we have touched upon in previous chapters.

A Lesson in Integrity

The greatest crisis facing human beings is not climate change or even the pandemic. It is a **lack of integrity**. The effects of disrespect and dishonesty are pervasive in our society. We see a lack of integrity from our political leaders, religious leaders, and corporate executives

Some of us remember the Enron debacle, Bernie Madoff, and most recently, large banks like Wells Fargo, Bank of America, and of course, Wall Street leading up to 2008. We have seen ongoing scandalous behavior from our supposed leaders and, most recently, religious institutions and even youth organizations. We see big businesses taking advantage of consumers. Corporations have made a fine art of it. Cheating has become too familiar, as evidenced by dozens of sports stars and entire sports teams (and state-sponsored Olympic programs) who use doping to get a competitive edge. The effects of disrespect and dishonesty seep almost invisibly into society's psyche to the point where almost nothing surprises anymore. The most damaging is that our youth are indoctrinated on the "win at all costs" mentality. The new norm has become a slippery slope.

As you continue your journey, you will undoubtedly notice it takes great courage to stand up for what one firmly believes. Even harder is not to judge others in a world that celebrates it. To hold fast and practice self-responsibility, perseverance, and humility is scarce indeed. Even rarer in today's society is acting in a way that puts others first by serving the greater good even when it is easier to do the exact opposite.

To be a total life warrior or total practitioner, one must live the art. It requires being congruent by walking your talk. The good news is if you truly walk the path (and walk your talk), it changes your life for the better in every area. It improves your:

- Confidence
- Personal Power
- Quality of Your Relationships
- Peace of Mind

- Awareness
- Ability to Get from Where You Are to Where You Want to go
- Ability to Live the Way You Want
- Overall Health

The key is to start now. Remember, there is no time like the present, and since life is present, to begin with, now is the time to act!

As John Boykin said, *"Time is life – nothing more, nothing less. The way you spend your hours and days is the way you spend your life."*

So how do you live honorably, you may ask? It's all about *clarity, commitment, and congruency. Most importantly, it's about integrity.*

A Person of Influence Has Integrity with People

Consider the following:

- ✓ Integrity requires consistency of character
- ✓ Absolute integrity is about the small things.
- ✓ Integrity is the foundation on which many other leadership attributes grow.
- ✓ Integrity is honesty accumulated
- ✓ Integrity commits itself to character over personal gain, principles over confidence, and the long view over immediate increase.
- ✓ Integrity is an inside job.

Too often, people compromise their integrity, losing themselves just for financial gain, control, or ego. Others compromise their integrity for a single spotlight moment. One of the reasons people struggle with integrity is that they tend to look outside of themselves to explain their character deficiencies. In other words, they blame others for their lack of integrity. It is always somebody else's fault.

That's not the way of the hero, warrior, or champion. It is not the way of the Master, and it's not for you. The hero journeying along the Master's Path understands that circumstances do not determine integrity. It is also not based on credentials or a title. Character comes from who you are at your core. Your core values help determine what you will stand for. It also helps determine what you will not stand for.

Your gut is where your moral compass lives. It is your connection to nature and everyone around you. The truth is you already know what to do. You have to have the courage to do it. I can't tell you how many people I have worked with over the years fail to recognize that their failures stem from their lack of courage to do right. That is, what is best for not only themselves but what is best for *all* parties involved. Here is what I know for sure. **The stronger your values are on the inside, the less validation and explanation are needed on the outside.**

"If I take care of my character, my reputation will take care of itself." – D. L. Moody

Courage is what distinguishes integrity from honesty, honor, and or ethics. It takes real courage to stand up for what is right, or fight injustice, whether it is easy, convenient, or profitable. Whether in business or on the battlefield, it is always best to lead with integrity.

Quest Challenge: Measure Your Integrity

Answer the following questions to help you measure your level of integrity.

- How well do I treat people from whom I gain nothing?
- Do I quickly admit wrongdoing without being pressed to do so?
- Do I put other people ahead of my best interest?
- Do I have an unchanging standard for moral decisions, or do circumstances determine my choices?
- Do I make difficult decisions, even when they have a personal cost attached to them?
- Am I honest with myself when it comes to the answers above?

If you are human, you most likely answered no to some of the questions above. Congratulations on being candid. Or perhaps you had to answer yes and no. You might have even written the word *sometimes*, which is probably the most accurate answer for most of us. No matter, the point of the exercise is to help you identify areas for improvement.

Integrity is honesty accumulated over <u>time</u> and builds or erodes <u>trust</u>

Good values establish Trust. The opposite is also true. When a person exhibits a lack of character, it erodes trust. Trust is needed between people to build solid relationships. It is the atmosphere in which people thrive.

How One CEO Taught His Employees A Lesson in Integrity

The following story by Carol Graham is worth remembering. It teaches why integrity is the key to living honorably. It also demonstrates how courage is the bedrock of living honorably.

A successful businessman was growing old and knew it was time to choose a successor to take over the business. Instead of choosing one of his directors or his children, he decided to do something different and called all the young executives in his company together.

He said, "It is time for me to step down and choose the next CEO. I have decided to choose one of you." The young executives were shocked as the boss continued. "I am going to give each one of you a seed today. This is one very SPECIAL seed. I want you to plant the seed, water it, and come back here one year from today with what you have grown from this seed. I will then judge the plants that you bring, and the one I choose will be the next CEO."

Jim, one of the executives, went home and excitedly told his wife the story. Together they got the pot, compost, and soil to plant the seed. Every day, he watered it and watched it closely to see the progress.

Three weeks went by, and the other executives were bragging about how well their seeds were growing. Every day, when Jim checked his pot, there was no sign of growth. After five weeks of this, Jim was pretty discouraged.

At the end of six months, Jim's pot remained empty - no sign of growth. He imagined he had overwatered it or got the wrong kind of fertilizer as his colleagues continued to brag about how tall their plants were growing; some of them were now trees.

NO growth after one full year.

The year was up, and they were instructed to bring their plants into the office for the CEO to inspect them. Jim told his wife how embarrassed he was to bring an empty pot to the office, but she encouraged him to be honest. Jim brought the pot to the board room and heard the snickers of the other executives. Their plants were a variety of shapes and sizes.

When the CEO arrived, he surveyed the room and greeted his young executives. Jim tried to hide in the back, totally embarrassed. The CEO was praising the executives for the growth and beauty of their plants.

"Today, I am pleased to announce that one of you will be my new CEO!"

The CEO asked Jim to come up from the front of the room, and Jim froze in fear that he was about to lose his job. Walking slowly to the front of the room, there was pity on the faces of the other executives as they imagined Jim was going to be fired.

The boss asked Jim what happened to his seed, and Jim told the story of how he nurtured and cared for the seed, but it never grew. The CEO then asked everyone to be seated except Jim as he announced, "I would like to introduce you all to your new Chief Executive Officer."

There were gasps and questions, "How can he be the new boss when his plant didn't even grow?"

The CEO explained, "One year ago, I gave everyone in this room a seed. What you did not know was that each seed had been boiled and was a dead seed. It was impossible for any of them to grow."

Jim was the only one in this room with the **courage and honesty** to bring me a pot with my seed in it. He did not substitute it with another seed as the rest of you did. Therefore, he has shown courage, honesty, and integrity, and I know he will run this company with a conscience."

The Benefit of Integrity: Trust

THE LINE OF COURAGE

As discussed, integrity builds trust and leads to influence. I call this walking the *Line of Courage*, as you learned in an earlier chapter. As you will learn in the next chapter, living honorably requires you to take the challenge, which requires courage in everything you do.

For now, suffice it to say there are eight simple steps you can take now to **build trust**. They are:

- ✓ Employ honest communications (speak from the heart and speak your truth)
- ✓ Value transparency
- ✓ Exemplify humility
- ✓ Demonstrate your support for others
- ✓ Fulfill your promises
- ✓ Embrace an attitude of service.
- ✓ Encourage two-way participation with the people you influence.
- ✓ Trust others by being clear in your expectations upfront

I want to leave you with several essential thoughts. First, when in doubt, ask yourself, "***Is this honest, and is this the best I can do?***" If you can answer honestly yes to the question, you are on the right path.

Quest Challenge: The Best Possible Solution

In your journal, answer the following three critical questions to ensure a win-win situation:

1. What is best for your student, client, or customer?
2. What is best for the community at large?
3. What is best for you or your organization?

The goal is to find a solution that resolves all three in a positive and caring way if possible. If you can do this, you are indeed living with honor.

I look forward to helping you even further on your journey along the Master's Path. The key is to stick with it and take the challenge covered in the next chapter.

Chapter 12

Taking the Challenge

This chapter is about taking the ultimate challenge along the Master's Path. You will learn the fundamental concepts of what I call the *almighty encounter*. It is what every hero, warrior, and champion must do to become a total practitioner. If you thoroughly learn and act upon the information contained in this chapter, you will be well on your way to reaching mastery. To do this, you must become aware of the fact that life is a test. Nothing is insignificant in your life. Every day is indeed an important day. Every second is a growth opportunity if you take the challenge.

The Ultimate Challenge – The Success Trifecta

THE SUCCESS TRIFECTA

Some life tests seem enormous and overwhelming, while others you don't even notice. Ultimately, all of them have implications as it regards what I call the *success trifecta*.

The **success trifecta** consists of three simple principles. They are:

1. Good health
2. Happiness
3. Love

The key to success is nothing more or less than good health, happiness, and love. Most people overlook the obvious, and they focus on the trivial or make things too complicated.

We will cover in detail ways to overcome trivial distractions along the Master's Path but also focus first on the many challenges you will face along the way. We will also focus on boiling things down to their very essence. In so doing, we will start to see that life doesn't have to be complicated.

Challenges in Life To Overcome

All life challenges fall into three basic categories. I am referring to the three significant assets. As you remember, they are *time, energy*, and *resources*. I am sure you have heard people say they don't have enough time, energy, or money. As you will see, most of the challenges listed below come down to a belief problem. They also come down to not using systems that make life easier.

"Don't wish it was easier, wish you were better. Don't wish for less problems, wish for more skills. Don't wish for less challenge, wish for more wisdom." – Jim Rohn

If life is a test, key principle number one is to achieve more by compressing time to achieve success faster. By doing this, you end up with more time to focus on the success trifecta. As an old mentor of mine used to say, "It's not more time but more intensity."

As I discussed earlier, we are all born with three significant assets. Time is the starting point where it all begins. Success compression is nothing more than using your time to focus on what is most important and avoiding all the distractions that come with the 21st Century.

➢ A Simple Example

I will use the analogy of a baseball game. Although we all love to see home runs and grand slams, most knowledgeable baseball fans realize the way to win the game is to hit a good number of singles and doubles. The occasional triple doesn't hurt either. Typically, the team that has the most hits wins. Life is like this. Incremental improvement is analogous to baseball hits. The goal is to move through the bases and make it home.

➢ A More Complex Example

The Apollo rocket that carried our astronauts to the moon back in 1969 used over 900,000 tons of rocket fuel for the trip. Most people don't know that more than half of the 900,000 tons went for take-off! Of course, Apollo leadership and the NASA engineering team understood this and believed without a doubt that a rocket ride to the moon was not only possible but very doable. They used the systems needed to ensure and compress time and with it achieve extraordinary success. Most importantly, they understood the amount of energy it would take to get started and successfully launch a rocket to the moon.

What's the lesson to be learned? It takes quite a bit of time and energy to get going, yet once we create inertia (the power of momentum), we start to see real gains, especially if we believe it is possible.

It takes a massive amount of energy to start something new. Much like building a snowball, it requires a bit of time and energy to take shape. It also involves inertia to get going, but once it does, momentum builds, and before long, the snowball effect kicks in. It grows with time and energy (velocity). It requires less energy to keep going and becomes nearly unstoppable once reaching the tipping point. We see this with avalanches where just a little bit of movement in the top layer of snow builds into something overwhelming.

Want another example? Think about a train in motion. It takes time and energy to get going, yet nothing better gets in its way once it has reached full speed. Accepting the challenge is no different for you and me. We must take the first step and keep going to gain velocity.

Energy and The Three Secrets of Success and Mastery

We become nearly unstoppable when we have a big enough purpose. Achieving great things requires a lot less energy in momentum when you have a big enough why behind it. Heroes, masters, and champions understand this and use it to their advantage. They start every endeavor with a big enough why.

Heroes also ask, "How will this affect my energy?" when presented with a decision to make. If achieving great things requires a good deal of energy, you are wise not to waste what energy you have. Remember that energy is like a muscle or a bank account for the mind, body, and spirit. You can either make a deposit or withdrawal. Using the example of an energy bank account, you have a choice to add to your energy by:

Mind

- Focusing on Positive Thinking
- Maintaining Peace of Mind
- Having an Attitude of Gratitude

Body

- Eating Healthy Food
- Drinking Pure Water
- Drinking Enough Water
- Exercising Regularly

Spirit

- Practicing Meditation
- Doing Breath Work
- Maintaining Positive Relationships
- Living Consciously and Intentionally
- Living by Design with Clarity (maintaining awareness)

Heroes also appreciate the *three secrets of success and mastery.* They utilize these to more quickly achieve the success trifecta. You too can apply the following **three mastery secrets**:

1. **Secret # 1** – Everything is energy, and **focus magnifies it** (**Energetic Determination**)

2. **Secret # 2** – Distractions **dissipate** energy (**Energetic Deviation**)

3. **Secret # 3** – Conserving and leveraging energy increases success, and **systems help** in the process (**Energetic Regulation**)

Secret #1: Energetic Determination

Your emotional well-being is often closely tied to your energy level. I call this the *E-Effect*. Let me give you a quick example using The Law of Control.

The Law of Control says, "You feel happy to the degree you think you are in control of your own life. Conversely, you feel unhappy to the degree to which you believe you are not in control of your own life.

Using energetic determination, when a person knows what they want, focuses on what they want, and follows up with targeted action, they are more fulfilled and happier emotionally. For example, a person who is clear on what they wish to accomplish, practices positive thinking, is grateful for what they have, is more likely to have peace of mind. If that person eats healthy food, is well hydrated with clean water, and exercises regularly, they are more apt to be healthy, happy, and emotionally balanced. Likewise, suppose that the same person meditates or prays regularly, develops positive relationships, and lives by design rather than chance. They will enjoy more, and a positive "*E-Effect*" will compound over time.

Secret #2: Energetic Deviation

An opposite *E-Effect* occurs when we allow or make withdrawals to our energy bank account. Using the Law of Control again, we can relate how our emotions become out of balance when we allow negative or "stinking" thinking into our lives. Fear, resentment, jealousy, or greed saps our energy. The same thing happens when we overeat junk food or try to ease our emotional pain with drugs/alcohol. I am sure everyone has experienced being around a negative person. They are energy vampires and suck the life right out of you. Each situation mentioned is a significant distraction and affects your energy and overall well-being. We see this happening on social media, with many living by default and allowing negative thinking to permeate their peace of mind and happiness. The same holds for those who are fixated on negative news.

Secret #3: Energetic Regulation

When a person lives on purpose instead of by default or chance, they increase their overall control and happiness. Modern psychology call this "Locus of Control Theory." Psychologists differentiate between an internal locus of control and an external locus of control. Your locus of control is where you feel the control exists in each area of your life. This location determines your happiness or unhappiness more than any other factor.

Someone with an internal locus of control feels they are the primary creative force in their own life. They prefer to make their own decisions and believe that everything happens to them for a reason. They understand that every action or behavior has a result. As a result, they live by successful habits that make them feel strong, confident, and happy. They think with greater clarity and perform at a higher level than the average person. They set empowering goals and work consistently towards achieving them. They are organized, persistent, and disciplined. They take time to rest when needed and know when to take a much-needed vacation. They use tried and true systems and procedures to multiply their results. They model the success of those who have proven themselves in their field of interest. They read and study what they need to learn, grow, share, serve, lead, and inspire.

The Most Important Skill in the 21st Century

Learning to control your attention and awareness to prevent distractions is key to success. Being busy is often nothing more than a lack of prioritization. Unfortunately, the truth is the human species is lazy. I don't mean to demean with this statement. It is just a fact for the majority of the world's population. Even the most successful achievers would prefer easy over hard. The goal is to think more intelligently, so you don't have to work harder unless you choose to. Never confuse activity with accomplishment, as stated in a previous chapter.

Have you ever said, "*I wish I had more time*" or, "*I just don't have time to do all the things I want to do*"? I'm sure we have all felt that way when the pressure's on, but here's the thing to remember. Time doesn't have to be linear. Complaining about time is about as pointless as complaining about gravity; it's a universal constant. The one thing you have in common with Jeff Bezos, Larry Page, Oprah Winfrey, Elon Musk, and Richard Branson is that you get 24 hours in a day.

If you are a leader, you no doubt have your share of challenges. It is your job to overcome them with proper solutions. You do this by setting up guidance or operations systems to help achieve the desired result. The key is to install the appropriate direction and operational systems into your daily life to maximize your time, energy, and resources.

Ways to Leverage Your Success

The super-successful use leverage to multiply their results. I just mentioned using the right tools and taking the time to plan it out before starting. Before looking at more specific strategies for multiplying your results, let us not forget to mention that heroes and highly successful people don't get it all done. Highly successful people <u>get the most important things done</u>. They prioritize and then concentrate on what is most important. The key is to find your vital functions and then focus on them.

185

Next, let's zoom out and look at leveraging skills at the macro level. Generally speaking, there are **six things to consider** when looking to leverage success. They are:

1. Start with the mindset (check your attitude)
2. Work harder when needed
3. Work more intelligently all the time
4. Work faster if called for (it is not more time but more intensity)
5. Work longer if needed
6. Work together (build teams)

Use Force Multipliers

Brian Tracy is one of my many mentors. I believe Brian Tracy borrowed a military principle (Force Multiplier) used to help smaller military forces leverage their recourses to defeat much larger military forces. Some of these best strategies are listed below.

Let's zoom in and look at **force multipliers** that work well in leveraging success. There are fourteen I recommend and use:

1. Decide in advance (DIA)
2. Skip Trivial Distractions
3. Create SMART Goals (Specific, Measurable, Attainable, Relevant, and Timebound)
4. Constantly check established deadlines (adjust as necessary and be flexible)
5. Get clear on priorities daily (**WIN** = **W**hat's **I**mportant **N**ow)
6. Value top performers (use incentives)

7. Delegate, don't abdicate
8. Educate (train up)
9. Work it only once if possible
10. Don't multi-task, instead multi-goal (combine goals)
11. Build an A-Team (utilize addition and multiplication)
12. Model Success (there is no reason to reinvent the wheel)

"Days are expensive. When you spend a day, you have one less day to spend. So, make sure you spend each day wisely."
– Jim Rohn

Quest Challenge: Using Force Multipliers

Take time now to create a list of your vital functions. Next, list leverage strategies you can apply today to multiply your results. To better help you:

- Go back through previous chapters and your notes and highlight your big takeaways.
- Flip through the pages of books you've already read and skim sections you've underlined and made notes in the margins.
- Look through notes you made on your phone or in Evernote while listening to powerful podcasts or reading an article online.
- Look back over your journals and re-read all your previous year's goals, plans, and resolutions.
- Look at all the bookmarks you've made, including powerful peak performance ideas you saved for future use.

- o Do an internet search for the vital functions of others super-achievers.
- o Study how the best leverage success.

The Art of Delegation

There are many ways to multiply your results which will help you with the challenges you face. One of the most effective is recruiting, hiring, and then delegating key areas you struggle with to other people who also believe in the vision, mission, and or project in front of you. For over forty-five years, I have had team members who have complimented my talents. God knows that what I received in particular skills, I lack in others. Fortunately, I learned that effective recruiting and delegating make the challenges faced more bearable. There isn't a day that goes by that this crucial skill set is not worth a fortune. It can not only make you a fortune but save you one as well.

My best advice is don't begrudge spending money to buy your freedom and bolster your success. No man or woman is an island. Also, keep in mind that you don't have to be in charge to be in control as an owner or entrepreneur. I was recently reminded of this crucial principle not long ago when I coached a client who could not give up control. He ultimately lost his business and his most prized staff because he could not give up control. The lesson is simple. Learn to delegate but don't abdicate.

I have found over the years that 80% of leaders attract followers. About 15% attract leaders. Only 5% of leaders *reproduce* leaders. Producing leaders takes time, energy, and resources. It also takes systems. It also requires that you have someone who is

Taking the Challenge

an excellent trainer who can help develop team members. They need to recognize, acknowledge, and encourage trainees and help them learn, grow, share, serve, lead, and eventually inspire. It is not easy, and yet the payoff is enormous.

Delegating tasks does not equate to less responsibility and making fewer decisions. As a hero and leader, you get *paid* to be responsible and make tough decisions. To "decide" in Latin means to "cut off" from the past. To grow is to change. The courage to decide is the job of the leader. It takes action even when the decision is not popular.

4 Things to Remember

There are four points I encourage you to keep in mind when being faced with a touch decision:

Pointer #1: Decide quickly. As Winston Churchill once said, "Once a decision is made, all agony goes away instantly." The best way to end the "agony" is to decide in advance and then take immediate action on your decision. Second-guessing rarely helps. Procrastination only prolongs the agony.

Pointer #2: Classify or categorize. Decisions come in two types. That is, those that can be reversed and those that can't. When making a decision that can't be reversed, you need to be sure before deciding. An example of a decision that can't be changed is an existential threat. Decisions that can be reversed are much more easily handled. For example, I often try to pilot or test decisions or projects before full implementation. We have a better chance of creating policies that will endure the test of time by seeing if they will fly first.

REVERSE OR BACK ENGINEERING

Pointer #3: You only need about 70% of the data to decide. I have found that most things I have to decide rarely come with all the answers in advance. Being human means, you live and learn as you travel the Master's Path. I believe hindsight is 20/20. The truth is you can't plot all the points all the time. Nor can you place all the pieces of the puzzle in one sitting. It takes time, energy, and often quite a few resources to get things exactly right. Welcome to the human condition. There is no substitute for experience. The closest I have found is finding world-class mentors who have walked the path before me. Fortunately, you can find world-class mentors if you look hard enough for them. I often find them while reading their bios, either in hard copy or on the internet. Here's what I have discovered - the most successful people quickly get started and then navigate along the way. Jeff Bezos of Amazon fame calls this **"best effort analysis."**

Pointer #4: Disagree and commit. It is okay to disagree – just don't be disagreeable. The truth is you can't build a team by being unpleasant. Nor can you win friends and influence people (i.e., lead) by being obnoxious. To teach and lead effectively, you need to be solution-oriented. Someone has to make a decision, and it needs to be the leader. The best leaders come up with the best solutions but can also effectively work with others to discover options not considered previously.

Teamwork and Leading Groups

If you happen to lead a group of people, you will no doubt occasionally find someone who chooses not to cooperate or be a team player. My best advice when this happens is to ask yourself the following questions:

1. Does this person add value to your life or that of the team?
2. Can I help this person?
3. If I can't help this person, is there someone who can? There needs to be a value proposition.
4. Is this worth my time, energy, and resources? If not, it may be time to move on.

You have one life to live. Your time is precious and fleeting. Use it wisely. You might even ask yourself if the challenge is worth your health, peace of mind, and happiness. If not, it may be time for a change. Don't get me wrong; you should try to do everything you can to help the situation. I also know that at some point, life is too short to focus on those who don't cooperate. As one of my mentors used to say, "Some do, some don't, so what." I prefer the saying, "Some do, some don't, some may still."

In the next chapter, we will focus on humility and perseverance. I will address some of the many effective techniques you can use to navigate tough decisions successfully in the next chapter. For now, let's look at some screening questions to help you further when taking the challenge.

Screening or Filter Questions

As you walk the Master's Path, you will find challenges and, with it, opportunities. It is part of the "Journey." As you have learned, if you pass the tests, you can continue forward and eventually reach the summit. If not, the "Journey" will be arduous at best. To avoid going in circles or backsliding, I encourage you to consider the following screening or filter questions:

Consider first your core values – For many who are reading, your core value consists of rock-solid beliefs and principles. The "Golden rule" comes to mind. That is, treat others like you want to be treated. Or, as discussed in an earlier chapter, perhaps you live by the "Platinum Rule." That is, treat others as they would like to be treated. In the martial arts, we live by a code, creed, and tenets that cover the pillars of honor. Whatever your core values are, I encourage you to screen your thoughts and actions accordingly. There is no doubt that heroes consider core values as a driving force in their lives.

Follow your strengths – We all have what one of my mentors calls our **area of competency**. In an earlier chapter, you might remember me explaining the circle of responsibility, including the top eight areas of your life. To review, your circle of responsibility is your health and fitness, finances, career or calling, education, spiritual life, friends and family, community or charitable works, and hobbies. Your area of competency includes your strengths. To better help you, I suggest you consider your sacred mission or significant purpose for being. I also encourage you to view your obligations. These are areas where you have given your word and committed for the "right reason." The Japanese word for this is "Geri."

We all have unique strengths and talents. If you are not sure, it may be time to figure it out. I encourage you to take the challenge and start working on it as a priority.

Consider outside counsel – I seek advice from those who have the experience to give it. I try to have world-class mentors in each area of my circle of responsibility, including my areas of expertise or competency. I try to seek advice from mentors with a "**proof positive**" track record. I look for the best in their field and then offer them something that adds value to the relationship. I encourage you to do the same. I also recommend that you avoid asking others to help you without first offering them something of higher value in return. It doesn't have to be monetary. It can be a service that brings us back to "Geri" or for the right reason. It can be helping them with an apprenticeship in your area of competency.

Trust your gut – We discussed the power of intuition in a previous chapter. Again, if it feels heavy, it probably is. If, on the other hand, *it feels light, it is probably right.* You will know if you listen carefully to your gut. Awareness is key. The power of intuition is unmistakable.

Quest Challenge: Face Life's Challenges

Take time now to answer the following questions in your journal:

1. What is your superpower?
2. How can you better take the challenge with the information (source code) in this chapter?
3. What is the one goal you have put off that will make the most significant positive impact on your life and those around you?
4. If you were 80 years of age and did not try to achieve the goal listed in number three above, would you regret it?
5. What would you regret the most if you didn't try it?

This chapter ends with the ultimate challenge, and that is to give your best and focus on excellence in everything you do. The question is: how do you maintain your best performance and **persevere**?

Chapter 13

The Power of Perseverance

In this chapter, you will learn how to stay on course for the long haul. It is what every hero, warrior, and champion must do to become a total practitioner. To do this, you must understand and act upon the most valuable skill of any leader and high-achiever. The skill to hone is stick-to-it-ness while maintaining focus. It will give you an unfair advantage in life, business, and success.

If you thoroughly learn and act upon the information contained in this chapter, you will be well on your way to reaching mastery and becoming a super achiever. Are you ready?

The Pursuit of Mastery

Most people underachieve in life because they do not realize how long it takes to achieve mastery in any field. From my experience, it takes at least 10,000 hours or approximately seven to ten years of hard work for you to move to the top of your field. For many, it may take ten to twelve years to get in the top 10%. What this means is simple. If you want to get in the top 10% of your field, you need to stay focused and stick with it for the long haul.

In my nearly 45 years of mentoring leaders, I have found that far too many miss the power of perseverance. It reminds me that time will pass anyway, so why not focus on becoming great at something. The question to ask yourself is, where will you be in five, seven, ten, or twelve years?

The good news is that if you set a goal, make a plan, and get clear on what you want, all you need to do is work long enough and stay focused, and you will eventually get there. Success in life requires perseverance. There is no substitute for stick-to-it-ness.

Remember this; if someone has achieved greatness, it took a lot of time, energy, and resources to get there. As I have often said to my students and clients, "Anything worthwhile takes a while." The fact that others have excelled in their area of interest is proof that you can as well. Your job is to put your head down, take action, and stick with it long enough for results to start showing up.

Attributes of Perseverance

There are nine attributes aka tools that will encourage you to persevere no matter what circumstance or challenge presents itself to you:

1) Definiteness of Purpose

As mentioned already, the super successful believe that everything happens for a reason, and it happens to serve them. The super successful have a **definiteness of purpose**. Let's take some time to zoom in on this potent attribute.

Would you like to enjoy more success and have less stress in your life? Do you wish that your daily aggravations had less power over you? Would you appreciate some more peace of mind? If you answered yes to any of these questions, there is good news. You don't need to find a genie in a bottle to enjoy these spectacular benefits. What you need is quite simple. First, you need to decide in advance why you exist and then believe without a doubt that everything happens to serve you. Things happen for a reason. Whether you already believe that things happen to help you or are unsure about this notion, here are some points to consider on being optimistic and solution-oriented rather than problem-oriented.

The super-successful don't curse their present circumstance or gripe about the past. When they encounter "negative" or stressful situations in their lives, they look for solutions rather than stay fixated on the problem. In contrast, champions and heroes look at every situation as an opportunity to learn and improve. Most people's immediate reaction is to be outraged, frustrated, or depressed when faced with a negative situation. Conversely, the super-successful focus on their definite purpose and look at challenges as stepping stones to success.

When you believe there's a purpose for your difficulties, your state of mind is quite different. You realize that your current situation is serving you somehow, whether it's a turn in the road or a lesson you can apply at a later date.

2) Desire – The Fire Within

I have been fortunate in my life to have met and mentored many super-successful people. I have also received mentoring from some of the best in their given field. What I have noticed is that they all share a **burning desire** to succeed. The champions, heroes, and super-successful all want it. The strong desire propels them over obstacles and through challenges. They rarely question their ability to overcome setbacks because their passion is so strong and their belief so great that they seem obsessed to many. The super-successful have a commitment and dedication to success which is stoked by the fire within. That fire is their <u>desire</u>, <u>passion</u>, and <u>definite purpose</u>.

3) Long Term Perspective

The super-successful know that the path is long, and it takes a **long-term perspective** to achieve great success. It takes time to learn and gain competence in any field. The true greats are those who kept their focus on the big picture. The big picture is a compelling vision. Short-term gain is excellent, and yet long-term focus brings lasting change. The long-term perspective is what brings winning traditions. History is full of examples of those who held a long-term view and were ultimately victorious because of it. Fads come and go, but masterpieces survive the test of time.

4) Willingness to Defer Gratification (Patience)

Patience is an attribute that all super-achievers have to learn. Super-achievers want things to happen quickly. It doesn't always come naturally to them. They are action-oriented. The truth is patience isn't passive; it is proactive. There is a process to it. Heroes, champions, and the super-successful understand that you can't cheat the process. As mentioned in previous chapters, there are often ways to compress success, but the truth is it takes time, energy, and resources to build or create a masterpiece.

Here are just a few areas where patience is essential:
- Mastering a skill

- Managing a project
- Navigating change
- Leading a business
- Building a marriage or lasting relationship
- Raising children
- Getting in shape
- Planning for retirement
- Becoming proficient at an instrument

5) Commitment to Lifelong Learning

Another critical habit that reinforces perseverance is **growth orientation**. Successful people understand that they must continually improve their knowledge, attitude, skills, and habits. This method of thinking and living is the foundation of success. I call it the success cycle for this very reason. It is cyclical as it ebbs and flows, and yet it lasts a lifetime if appropriately practiced.

6) An Attitude of Gratitude

The habit of **feeling and expressing gratitude** also reinforces perseverance. By being thankful for all you have and saying it regularly, one sees life as a gift. You begin to realize that even challenges are opportunities to become better. When you become grateful for the challenges, you soon see life as a test. You either pass the test, or you hopefully learn from it. Either way, you see everything as an opportunity to learn, grow, share, serve, lead, and inspire.

There are many benefits to an attitude of gratitude that makes your journey along the Master's Path more enjoyable and more productive. An attitude of gratitude makes you a warmer, friendlier, and more genial person. It also helps you to be more sensitive and aware of the people around you. An attitude of gratitude also gives you a sense of happiness, inner satisfaction, and a feeling of expectation of what is coming next. Here is what I have learned. The more gratitude you have, the more gratitude you express. The more gratitude you speak, the happier you seem to be. The happier you seem to be, the better and more positive is your personality. The more positive your personality, the higher your self-esteem, and the better you can handle the challenges that will inevitably come your way.

Another benefit of an attitude of gratitude is it helps heighten your creativity. How may you ask? The answer is an attitude of gratitude helps unlock your unconscious or what some call your sub-conscious mind. The super successful know that the ultimate creative force is located somewhere beyond our everyday consciousness. Whether you call this the subconscious mind, the universal mind, or infinite intelligence (God), the most successful people tap into this source to generate creative ideas. The super successful also understand the quickest way to tap into this source of power is through an attitude of gratitude.

7) Humility

There is an inner peace that comes with being battle-tested over the long haul. Win some, lose some, and in the end, you realize that you are doing well if you have a few more "W's" than "L's." As Ralph Waldo Emerson said, "All Life is an experiment. The more experiments you make, the better." You will find the more successful the person, the more humble they are as they know what it is like to fail.

If you think about it, experiments are essentially a test. Experiments are tests to discover an outcome. There's a test and then a result. Some turn out well, and some don't. The key is not to give up and remain humble in the process. See failure as it is - that is, just another opportunity to learn and grow.

8) Understanding the Laws of Nature

We see the importance of **perseverance in nature** all the time. The seasons teach us there is a time for everything and everything for a time. Take the mighty oak tree for example. It starts as an energy package that we call a seed or acorn. The seed takes hold in good soil, and with time it starts to grow. With time, sun (energy), rain, the seed grows, and roots form. With more time and some struggle or resistance, the roots take hold, and more growth occurs. The roots start to expand, and soon, the tree begins its visible growth upwards. With more time, some more struggle (wind/storms, etc.), the tree grows further upwards and soon starts to produce branches, blossoms, and eventually more seeds. The process is unmistakable. And it takes time, energy, and resources.

A similar process to the mighty oak is evident in growing a business. First, you must prepare for success by proper planning. It takes time and energy. Next, you need to invest in the necessary resources to help your business grow. It takes adequate training and development. It often requires an apprenticeship. It would help if you then learned all aspects of running a business, including sales, marketing, administration, basic accounting, and team building, to name a few. I am sure you get the idea. The bottom line: it takes patience and over the long haul to grow something worthwhile.

9) Enduring Focus

The most valuable attribute for mastering perseverance is a **focus that endures**. As stated earlier, we live in a time of great distraction. The super-successful are masters of keeping their focus and mastering the mundane—heroes, champions, and the super-successful use many techniques to keep their focus. We have discussed some of these already. For example, deciding in advance and clarifying your vision, mission, and values are essential. So too are writing down SMART goals and revisiting them frequently. Success strategies such as the **Pareto Rule** and finding **leverage points** help us focus and maximize our potential. Understanding and using proper time management, energy management, and resource management also helps. Gamifying the boring also helps.

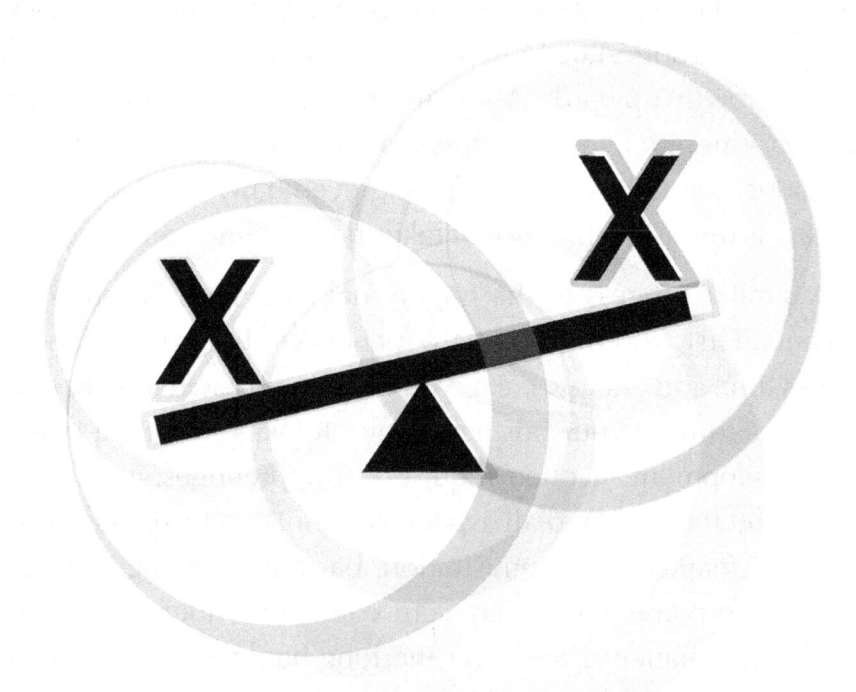

LEVERAGE POINTS & POWER OF MULTIPLICATION

When you gamify your life, you make work novel and fun. Journalizing your significant accomplishments as part of the journey along the Master's Path is an example. You may have discovered that nothing captivates human attention and engagement like a game. I figured this out years ago when I was responsible for teaching children martial arts. Nothing would keep their attention better than making a game out of what children could consider boring. We have a name for this in the martial arts industry. It is called the art of disguising repetition. As adults, we all realize that to master anything; you have to master the mundane. The truth is that to master anything, whether it be in the martial arts or any field, you must constantly practice the fundamental basics. Think about it. A master musician on any instrument is continually practicing the essential scales.

Of course, keeping one's focus is not always easy. It takes discipline, willpower, and the ability to keep your eye on the prize.

The Power of Stick-to-it-ness and Willpower in the Face of Fear

I will never forget the first time I scuba-dived. We were in the British Virgin Islands. It was 1995, and my wife and I joined some dear friends to rent a sailboat from The Moorings in Tortola. While sailing from one beautiful island to the next, I decided I would like to dive the Wreck of the Rhone. The only problem was that I never had scuba-dived, so I paid for a resort course. I came to learn that a resort course is typically a few hours long, consisting of a lecture, some pool work (or, in this case, the shallow water off the resort's property where you can stand). The whole idea of the course was to get acquainted with the equipment and then complete a dive or two. Typically, the first dive can be a shore dive or a boat dive. In our case, the resort course lasted about one hour and consisted of learning how to clear our dive masks if we got water in them. The instructor also showed us how to use the regulator to breathe underwater correctly. I was surprised I passed the course, yet I suspect everyone does if they pay for the lesson. I could barely clear my mask and had done it only once in shallow water. Our instructor seemed pleased with our progress, yet I wasn't confident in my ability after such a short course.

We left the resort on a boat to take our first dive in about 20 to 30 feet of water. After getting our equipment situated, our instructor told us to be careful of "fire coral." He said it would be red and it would burn and be very painful if we touched it. With that pleasant thought in our minds, we followed our instructor overboard and down a rope line to what appeared to be an underwater rock and coral labyrinth. My wife didn't like the experience of being underwater and quickly turned around to go back up the rope line to the boat. After making sure she was okay with a thumbs up, I continued following the instructor. We were swimming between a maze of rocks and coral, and I was not paying close enough attention as I looked out for fire coral. Unfortunately, I had floated too close to my instructor's fins, and one of them hit my mask and knocked it nearly off. I started to panic with fear as I wasn't comfortable with clearing my diving mask. Add to this the fact that I was at least 25 feet underwater, and I couldn't see well without it; I panicked even more. As I frantically tried to put my mask back on and clear off the saltwater, I turned around and hit fire coral. The sting to my leg was like being poked with a fireplace iron. I was now in full panic as my instructor swam ahead, oblivious to my situation.

The Power of Perseverance

The thought crossed my mind that this might be my last moment as a living, breathing human being. I could only think of one thing: to swim as fast as possible to the surface. In a panic to get to the surface, I spat out my mouthpiece regulator and took in a whole mouth full of saltwater. Despite the fear, I somehow made it to the surface and must have looked like a rocket breaking the surface. I gulped up my first full breath of air and thought how lucky I was to have survived.

Meanwhile, our instructor surfaced to check on me. He didn't seem overly concerned, which honestly made me a bit mad. To say I wasn't in the mood to continue with my scuba diving experience in the Caribbean would be the understatement of the year. When our instructor told me that I would be fine and that I needed to follow him back down, I told him in no uncertain terms that I wasn't going to happen. I explained my leg was still burning from the fire coral, and I felt lucky to be still alive.

The instructor then said something I will never forget. He said, "Mr. St. James, if you don't go back down and complete this dive, you will never dive again, and that would be a real shame." I knew he was right, and despite my better judgment, I followed him back down and completed the dive. Fortunately, I had only grazed the fire coral, and my leg had stopped burning. I was sure to stay well behind the instructor, and he did a better job of keeping an eye out for me. I not only survived the dive, but I also ended up enjoying it once I got over the initial scare.

I am happy to report that I did indeed dive the Wreck of the Rhone that same trip. I not only enjoyed it, but I also had to be corralled by the dive guide as we were supposed to stay together at the top half of the wreck (the bow), which sat on the sea bed at about 40 feet. The impact site was in two parts. The stern was in about 85 feet of water. The slope down between the two was gradual enough that I hadn't noticed it. I had dived to nearly 80 feet to get to the stern. Fortunately, I survived that experience and eventually dived the Great Barrier Reef with some close students and friends in 2007 in Australia. It was an experience I will never forget.

The moral of the story is quite simple. You have to get back on the horse or, in this case, take a deeper dive after facing your fear. Perseverance requires facing the terror barrier and overcoming it. Whether it is public speaking, skiing, motorcycle riding, scuba diving, rock climbing, or martial arts, you will have to break through mental barriers to build a better future along the Master's Path.

FEAR is an obstacle all heroes overcome. But they also have to pay the price.

Paying the Price

When I speak about paying the price, I am talking about the power of persistence. The reality is heroes recognize that everything worthwhile is a struggle. Everything you have ever wanted is uphill, as my friend and mentor John C. Maxwell often states.

Two words come to mind when we speak about paying the price. One is a purpose, and the other is hard work. The super-successful have a love or passion for their purpose. The super-successful have a passion for their purpose that borders on an obsession and is real power. They pursue their goal at almost any cost. At this stage, persistence becomes the primary factor in their success. The great ones know that the longer they work and the harder they work, the more successful they will become. Champions decide in advance what they want, down to great detail, and then wage war to get it. Quitting is not an option. Their dogged persistence and a sense of passion and purpose are the fuel that gets them from where they are to where they want to be. The super-successful hope for success, and yet they do more than hope. They take massive action daily to ensure they move the ball down the field. This winning expectation is the fuel that drives the champion to persist until they succeed. The belief that pain is nothing more than an indicator of progress is common to all who endure and reach for the stars.

Quest Challenge: Know Where You Stand

Take time now to "know" where you stand. Answer the questions below:

1. How long am I willing to experience pain to get from where I am to where I want to go?
2. Am I willing to experience a little pain, a fair amount, or whatever it takes to get from where I am to where I want to be?
3. Do I love what I do, and am I willing to do it even when the going gets tough?

Before proceeding to Chapter 14, I want to leave you with a quote that bears a harsh truth, but that also might empower you to "toughen up" and persevere while on your journey:

"To succeed in life, one must have the determination and must be prepared to suffer during the process. If one isn't prepared to suffer during the adversities, I don't really see how he can be successful." Gary Player – Professional Golfing Legend

Chapter 14

The X Factor of Success: Growth Mindset with the Discipline of the Master

In this chapter, I want to reveal to you the X-Factor of Success. We will take a deep dive into what it takes to become a hero and learn that it takes the discipline of a Master to make it happen. To do this, you must understand and act upon the most valuable skill of any leader and high-achiever. The skill to hone is developing a **growth mindset**. You will discover that it takes consistency of study and ongoing application to make it happen. Demonstrating these qualities will give you an unfair advantage in life, business, and success. If you thoroughly learn and act upon the power of a growth mindset reinforced by consistency, you will be well on your way to developing the discipline of the Master.

The # 1 Key to Your Future – Growth Mindset

The number one key to your future is having a **growth mindset**. You know by now that the Japanese term for this is *Kaizen*, better known by the acronym **CANI** or Constant And Never-Ending Improvement.

The truth is we are all in the human development business. If you are on the journey to life mastery, you are focused on personal growth first and foremost. I like to tell my clients, "It's not what you get but instead what you become." It is about becoming your best at the end of the day. It is about personal growth. It is also about developing your fullest potential, mind, body, and spirit.

Don't mistake being positive-minded as growth-minded. It is possible to be positive and not grow. It comes down to tangible improvement. If you are not improving daily, you are falling behind.

"It's not the strongest of the species that survives, nor the most intelligent that survives. It is the one that is most adaptable to change." Charles Darwin

The ability to constantly adapt, adjust, and tweak one's approach is part of the DNA of all super-achievers.

Fixed Mindset

No matter where you are now, you can always grow in the future with a growth mindset. Conversely, a fixed mindset is a death nail in the 21st Century. It is self-sabotage.

Having a fixed mindset is a sign of living in your comfort zone. The truth is the object of a fixed mindset is to look good, feel good, be right, or be in control. We referred to these in a previous chapter as the **four big payoffs**.

The only variable that will determine your success is your mindset – a growth mindset. The fixed mindset says, "It wasn't

Growth Mindset with the Discipline of the Master

meant to be" when faced with perceived failure. You will also hear, "It is what it is," or "It wasn't in the cards." The person with a fixed mindset consistently underperforms. The person with the growth mindset challenges themselves to learn, grow, share, serve, lead, and inspire. The ability to adapt and overcome is the hallmark of the super-successful.

Your mindset is the source code behind all your behaviors, actions, and reactions to everything that happens in your world.

Self Identity SetPoint (S.I.S.P.)

To a large extent, we are all controlled by our **self-identity set point**. Self-identity is how you identify and define yourself. Your self-image includes a combination of personality traits, abilities, physical attributes, interests, hobbies, and social roles from your identity that you specifically selected to identify yourself.

Your set point is where you are most comfortable. Much like a thermostat, you are most comfortable with those things you know. Think about it in terms of the **Success Cycle** which we have defined previously as being made up of your knowledge, attitude, skills, and habits (**your K.A.S.H.**). Your set point is your personal development at a certain point in time. Your current stasis is where you are most comfortable. When things become heated due to new challenges, new information, and or other types of changes or perceived changes, your mental thermostat or self-identity set point kicks in. Like the temperature in your home, the air conditioning kicks in if it gets to 78 and is too hot. Likewise, if the temperature drops to 65, the heat kicks in. The goal is to bring you back to the point of comfort, which we call the comfort zone. The process is called ***homeostasis***, or the tendency toward a relatively stable equilibrium or balance. It is not only seen in physiological functions but also in psychological conditioning.

Your self-image develops during your formative years. As children, our parents, teachers, coaches, family, and friends helped to set it. It is your job to develop your setpoint while developing your fullest potential. If you are a leader, it is also your job to raise your team's setpoint continually. Remember, you don't achieve goals; you grow into them. By placing the setpoint on what you want, your growth mindset rises to the occasion. It is why the most significant investment you can ever make is on growth and personal development. If you lead a team, your best asset is creating a setpoint of excellence and providing the training and development necessary to make it happen.

If you look at this process as a journey, you'll see that it's really about self-improvement or, better yet, about what you and your team can become. Becoming better every day is really what the journey is all about. It is about constant and never-ending improvement. To have more, you must first be and do more. You must improve your knowledge, attitude, skills, and habits.

"The aim of life is to see what all you can become with all you have been given." – Jim Rohn

Understand that virtually anyone that has climbed to the top of their field has failed forward. Somewhere in their lives, they, like you and me, decided that they were going to be the best they could be and were willing to learn the knowledge and master the skills necessary to climb to the top of their field. It was a matter of choice. It was also an investment of time, energy, and resources.

Throughout time, there's one idea that has held. The world's greatest thinkers, philosophers, psychologists, theologians, and

Growth Mindset with the Discipline of the Master

experts in the field of personal development have come to accept that the one key factor that determines a person's success is their self-image. How you see yourself is how you see the world. When your self-image is high, you see opportunities rather than problems. You see challenges as a test to pass rather than an obstacle to prevent you from moving forward. You look for solutions to better serve humanity.

The good news is your self-image can change and, with it, your trajectory. You can raise your setpoint and experience the joy of transformation. The bad news is unless you are aware of how conditioning works, it is too easy to fall back into your comfort zone. You can never grow beyond your self-image and, with it, your setpoint.

Take, for example, a person who is used to barely getting by. They then win the Mega-Million lottery and start buying things they never had, which will make them feel like a "million." We have all seen it before. First, they buy a big home or mansion. Next, it is one, two, or several luxury cars. Of course, they need the latest and most fabulous luxury items to fill up their new digs. They continue spending like there is no tomorrow, and before long, they are broke and don't know what happened.

You also see the opposite of this. A person who has a high self-image and is fit physically. They gain weight over the holidays or during a period of stress or crisis. They see themselves in the mirror and or feel the extra pounds when they try to exercise. Their clothes are too tight, and it doesn't take long for their internal thermostat to kick in. Their self-identity setpoint (S.I.S.P.) is not at all comfortable with what is going on. It doesn't take long for them to shed the weight and get back in shape. Most importantly, it doesn't take long for them to get back in alignment and congruent with their conditioned self-image.

We also see this in the business world. Someone who is otherwise successful tries a new venture and fails in the attempt. The temporary setback isn't congruent with the self-image and S.I.S.P. Before long, they are back up and building lasting success. This is why the world's best coaches and consultants focus on self-image first and foremost.

> *"I see life almost like a long university education that I never had. My interest in life comes from setting myself huge, apparently unachievable challenges and trying to rise above them."* – Sir Richard Branson

Again, there is good news. You can change your setpoint. The bad news is you will never have the health, wealth, happiness, and or love beyond your self-identity setpoint.

There are many ways to build a winning self-image and with it raise your setpoint. What follows are some of my favorites:

- Build empowering belief first
- Have the right intention
- Demonstrate a strong desire
- Learn less and study more
- Take massive action
- Check your results by tracking progress (the power of precision)
- Say "yes" to new experiences
- Say "no" to negotiating
- Develop creativity

Growth Mindset with the Discipline of the Master

- Capture courage
- Master discipline

Raise your setpoint and do the work, and you are very near to becoming a full-fledged Master.

Develop Your Top 12 Attributes

I was overseeing a leadership symposium recently on Zoom we call our annual "Master's Clinic." During the two-day event, I was honored to share my thoughts with our Master's Path candidates. During this segment, I asked the group to help me develop what they considered to be the top twelve attributes of someone who has mastered their craft.

As I started to ask our attendees their thoughts, the group soon realized the challenge was paring the list back to a top twelve. For example, here is a portion of the attributes we came up with to better help you discover what you feel are most important – you can even print this out and use it as a checklist:

- ☐ Someone aware
- ☐ A person with a robust belief system
- ☐ A focused person
- ☐ A person of courage
- ☐ Someone determined
- ☐ Someone energetic and enthusiastic
- ☐ A person who is open-minded and flexible in their thinking
- ☐ A person with a growth mindset who is goal-oriented
- ☐ Someone who demonstrates admirable character and honor

- [ ] Someone who is inspired to give their best always
- [ ] An action-oriented person
- [ ] Someone creative
- [ ] A patient person
- [ ] Someone who is purposeful
- [ ] A person who is willing to persevere
- [ ] Someone caring and conscientious
- [ ] A team player
- [ ] Somebody who is humble
- [ ] A person who is ambitious (hungry) and or a self-starter
- [ ] Someone authentic
- [ ] A person who is fun or humorous
- [ ] A person with good follow-up and follow-through
- [ ] A good communicator
- [ ] A good listener
- [ ] Someone who is quality conscious and precise
- [ ] A passionate person
- [ ] Someone who takes ownership of their behavior and work
- [ ] A resourceful person
- [ ] A person of discipline
- [ ] A person with a fast response time

We could have kept going, but we only had so much time, and I wanted the group to take a deep dive and check to see which ones they felt were the most important. I also thought it essential to consider which twelve were most common among our group. Of course, there were no wrong answers, only food for thought.

Quest Challenge: Defining Your Top Attributes

Take time now to answer the following questions.

1. Which of the above do you consider to be the essential attributes of success?
2. What are your top three attributes?
3. What are your top ten or twelve attributes?
4. How could you use this powerful exercise with your team if you lead a team?
5. Are you a living example of your top 10 to 12 attributes?

Taking Inventory Along the Path

When we think about a growth mindset, it is vital to remember that it is not more information but *more application*, as mentioned in a previous chapter. We need to learn less and study more. Let me explain.

It is not about gaining knowledge for the sake of just acquiring knowledge. Instead, it is about taking a deep dive and studying what you have learned to the point you can apply it practically to your life. The goal is to move from the constant consumption of information and knowledge to mastery of the skills necessary to take it to the next level and beyond.

I am sure we have all met the over-motivated underachiever who is all talk and no action. You know the ones. They are all excited to start but never finish. They buy all the stuff and yet never put it to use. The fitness industry caters to this type of person. There are large name fitness chains that bank on this type of mentality. It is not about quality but rather quantity. The strategy is to sell a low monthly contract with unlimited use of the facility and count on the fact that the new member will only come for several months before losing interest.

If you are reading this book and are a seeker, I hope you will take inventory of what we have covered thus far. I hope you will do more than read the many great ideas, options, systems, and strategies contained herein. I want you to grow by using the information daily. To better help you, I am listing some of the essential concepts offered thus far. I hope you will study them until you can apply them.

Your Application Checklist: Actionable Content from the Master's Path

- ☐ Kaizen – Constant and Never-Ending Improvement Mentality (A Growth Mindset)
- ☐ The Law of Awareness (Self, Situational, and Heightened)
- ☐ Taking A.I.M.
- ☐ The STAR Formula
- ☐ Being an Observer
- ☐ Gap Analysis
- ☐ Tracking
- ☐ Living Intentionally
- ☐ Seeking Satori
- ☐ The Compound Effect
- ☐ The Success Trifecta
- ☐ The Success Cycle
- ☐ The Success Paradigm

GROWTH MINDSET WITH THE DISCIPLINE OF THE MASTER

- ☐ The Power of Paradigms
- ☐ The Line of Courage
- ☐ The Circle of Responsibility
- ☐ W.I.N. Principle
- ☐ The Pareto (80/20) Rule

THE PARETO (80/20) RULE

- ☐ The 4 Payoffs of Human Nature
- ☐ The Beginner's Mindset – "Shoshin" or the Power of E
- ☐ Rinse and Repeat
- ☐ The Terror Barrier – Stepping Out of Your Comfort Zone
- ☐ Do the Thing and Have the Power
- ☐ Possibility Thinking – Think Out of the Box

POSSIBILITY THINKING – THINK OUT OF THE BOX

- [ ] Reverse or Back Engineering
- [ ] The Great Assets (Time, Energy, Resources)
- [ ] Understanding Energy
- [ ] Energetic Determination
- [ ] Energetic Deviation
- [ ] Energetic Regulation
- [ ] The Law of the Lid
- [ ] The Law of Contribution
- [ ] Leadership Core Competencies
- [ ] Emotional Intelligence vs. I.Q.
- [ ] Understanding Time
- [ ] Time and Success Compression

TIME AND SUCCESS COMPRESSION

- ☐ Strategic Planning
- ☐ Warrior or Hero Tactics
- ☐ An Empowering Vision

AN EMPOWERING VISION

- ☐ Your Sacred Mission
- ☐ Understanding Resources
- ☐ The Mastermind
- ☐ Leverage Points & Power of Multiplication
- ☐ Force Multipliers
- ☐ Gamification

GAMIFICATION

- ☐ The Power of Perseverance & Precision (enduring focus)
- ☐ The X-Factor of Success
- ☐ A Growth Mindset
- ☐ The discipline of the Master
- ☐ Spiritual Gift of the Artist

In the next chapter, I will take you a step deeper into what it takes to actualize the X-Factor of Success and how to become a true Master.

Chapter 15

The Discipline of the Master

You have experienced quite a journey thus far. I want to congratulate you on your perseverance and commitment to making it up to this chapter. Most readers won't. Most readers aren't ready for it. If this book means more to you than another addition to your bookshelf, then please pay very close attention to these final two chapters, which are pivotal to fully succeeding on your journey along the Master's Path.

In this next chapter, we will focus on the other essential component of the X-Factor of Success; **the discipline of the Master**.

Consistency Is Key

The number one cause of failure is a **lack of consistency**. It is the Achilles heel of success. I have seen it time and time again as a master instructor or coach. Most people make promises and set goals, but few follow up. One of my many mentors, John C. Maxwell, describes it this way. He said, "everyone starts but few finish, and even fewer finish well." The major reason for this is what some call *drift*, or what we are calling a lack of consistency.

Today, we have social media, streaming television and movies, and powerful smartphones, Apple watches, and no shortage of other electronic distractions. The result is even more drift, or what I called earlier energetic deviation. Distraction dissipates energy and, with it, focus and commitment.

Commitment is nothing more than doing the thing you said you were going to do, long after the mood you said it in had left you. It is the ability to stick with it even when the going gets tough. We have all heard the Aesops fable, "The tortoise and the hare." Slow and steady are attributes that work well if speed and stamina are not an option for success.

Lack of consistency is the subtle destroyer of all progress, goals, and dreams. It kills momentum every time.

Quest Challenge: Consistency Scoring

I want you to open up your journal and create two columns – one for daily/consistent habits you want to acquire and one for what habits you actually employ during your day.

If you list, say, eight habits you want to acquire, then assume that as eight points. Now look to the other column; have you listed eight habits you act upon daily there?

Another important thing to consider is that you cannot add value to a habit that is a duplicate of another habit. For example, "working out" can translate to various tasks ("lifting weights", "running three miles a day", etc) but each task is part of the general umbrella of "working out".

How much are you scoring over on the "habits I employ daily" column? And what habits can you add to that list so that they apply to each desired habit in the other column?

You can also take time to answer the following questions:

1. Are you consistent in your behavior, habits, attitude, and communication?
2. Do you walk your talk even when it is easier to do otherwise?
3. What success routines or rituals do you use daily (and are they all listed in the relevant column)?

The Power Belt

In the mid-90s, a friend of mine who owned an industrial design firm was a co-owner of the Power Belt. I believed that the product, which was designed for walkers, could be used in martial arts. After seeing and working with the Power Belt team, I told my friend that I thought it could help martial artists train more effectively by offering resistance to their punches and blocks. The owners agreed and asked me if I would like to market the Power Belt to the martial arts industry.

I decided to seek out some experts in the martial arts industry to get their input. To make a long story short, I flew to Los Angeles and met with Billy Blanks, Cathy Long, and Benny "the Jet" Urquidez all on the same day. It was quite the 24-hour adventure, including my flight out there.

When I arrived at Burbank Airport, I was greeted by a black belt member of the organization I belonged to at that time. It was a tradition that, when a Master instructor arrived in your area, you would greet them at the airport in "dress blues," a navy-blue business suit with a proper dress shirt and association tie. The fellow who greeted me was a 2nd-degree black belt and looked the part when I approached. He bowed with profound respect, and people in the airport started to look to see what was going on. My greeter looked like an official delegate or bodyguard meeting a dignitary. From there, the journey began.

Our first stop was to attend Billy Blanks's "Tae Bo" class. In the late 1980s, Blanks developed the Tae Bo workout while running a karate studio in Quincey, Massachusetts. He used components of his martial arts and boxing training. Mr. Blanks opened a fitness center in Los Angeles to teach his new workout. He later attracted celebrity clients such as Paula Abdul and the comedian Sinbad. I met Sinbad while waiting to get into the studio for the morning workout. The popularity of the activity quickly grew, becoming a pop culture phenomenon after Blanks began releasing mass-marketed videos.

I will never forget waiting for 30 minutes in a line to get in. Over 100 people, including celebrities, were hanging around waiting for Billy's morning workout. I jumped in the back of the class when it started and was dripping wet when it was over.

Mr. Blanks agreed to a quick one-on-one meeting after the workout when I showed him the Power Belt. He asked me to follow him into the gym's weight lifting section when he said, "who's your bodyguard?" I explained he was just a friend, and from there, I presented the Power Belt. He put it on and tried it and said it had potential and then gave me a few pointers, which I greatly appreciated. As he used the product, I asked him about his training regimen, and he lit up like a kid in a toy store. We spoke for about 15 minutes, and I thanked him for his time.

It was then time to meet Cathy Long and train in her class on the other side of town. For those who don't know who Cathy Long is, she is an American kickboxer, mixed martial artist, and actress. She has held various kickboxing championships, including two KICK World Kickboxing titles and the W.K.A. and I.S.K.A. world titles. To say Cathy was fit when I trained in her class would be an understatement.

Cathy's class was held in a huge fitness center in L.A. Imagine no less than 25 large, heavy bags hanging from the rafters, and you will start to get an idea of the type of class that Ms. Long taught. We spent well over an hour hitting the bags after starting with a good warm-up. I will never forget her coming up to me and saying, "you have good technique." She then asked, "what are you aiming for?" I told her the middle of the bag. She then taught me something I will never forget. She said when she trains; she typically aims for either the "R" or "L" in "Everlast," which was the brand name emblazoned across every bag. She then smiled and said, "give it a try and tell me what you think."

Cathy was fluid and yet powerful in her moves. After the workout, I asked her if she had a moment to check out a product I had. She was gracious and asked me if she could try it. She then worked with the Power Belt as Billy Blanks had before her. She did some jabs, crosses, hooks, and uppercuts. When done, she gave me a couple of tips and said she would be interested in getting a Power Belt. I gave her my card and thanked her for her time, and then it was off to meet Benny "The Jet" Urquidez.

The Masters Path

Benny Urquidez is an American kickboxer, martial arts choreographer, and actor. He was a non-contact karate competitor who later pioneered full-contact fighting in the United States. He had opened a gym in Los Angeles years before our meeting, and it was a hub for anyone wanting to get ready for a serious fight. Mr. Urquidez was called the "The Jet" for many reasons, not least of which was his blinding hand speed and devasting thrust kicks. He was small in stature but built like a locomotive when I met him. He was in the ring sparring when I arrived.

The facility was large, with several rings and no shortage of heavy bags hanging from the rafters—the smell of sweat was pungent in the air. There were weights and other training equipment, yet "the ring" was where the action was. So it was that I waited patiently for a break in the action when I stepped ringside and introduced myself.

Benny looked down and said, "how can I help you?" I asked if I could have a minute of his time to show him a product and lifted the Power Belt towards him. He said, hop on in, and you can show me what it does. I was excited to jump in the ring with Benny "The Jet" Urquidez but at the same time hoping I was not his next sparring partner. Fortunately for me, he only wanted to see what the Power Belt was all about. After I demonstrated some hand combinations, he said, "Interesting, may I try?" He then took it and proceeded to go through his favorite hand combinations. He looked at me and said, "it needs a vest to go with it." I asked him what he meant, and he said, "the resistance bands need to go through a torso vest to ensure maximum efficiency." He was, of course, right. He had studied karate and full-contact fighting for many years and knew his craft well, primarily what works when training for maximum power, speed, and precision.

The Discipline of the Master

I thanked Mr. Urquidez for his gracious time and gave him my card. He told me the next time I was back to stop in and join him in the ring for some sparring. I remember saying something like, "thank you, Sir, it would be my pleasure." It would have been fantastic to train with him, yet my only full-contact fighting to that point was done in Tijuana, Mexico, at open Karate competitions. Technically, the tournaments were supposed to be non-contact, but no one used safety gear, and the rules were loose. It was an unwritten rule that the black belt division was an open game, and full contact was expected with only a knockout ending up in a D.Q. or disqualification.

As my assistant was driving me back to the airport, I remember him looking at me and saying, "That was amazing." He went on to say, "It is incredible the way each person you met with gave you their time and shared their thoughts openly." I told my friend that "Masters" love to talk about their passion. I explained all you need to do is ask and listen. I learned what I needed. I remember thinking that it was all about personal growth and the discipline of the Master.

All three martial arts legends were students first, Master instructors second, and entrepreneurs third. Each was at the top of their game. That is the game of life. Each one had consistently practiced their discipline for many years and honed their skills in actual combat. Each was charismatic and open to sharing the love of their art. Each possessed real power, precision, and persistence. They had the attributes needed to be successful wherever they focused. Each one was on a hero's journey along the Master's Path.

As we continue our epic journey, take time to dig deep. Take action on the ideas, options, systems, strategies, tactics, and techniques explored to date in this book. Continue to work towards the progressive realization of your worthy goals. Check yourself constantly to make sure you are still a student first and foremost. Hone your knowledge, attitude, skills, and habits, and know I look forward to seeing you along the Master's Path.

Chapter 16

The Spiritual Gift of the Artist

"Excellence is the highest form of power we can achieve as a human being." - Robert Green

Welcome to the final and most spiritually inclined chapter of the book, where we will discuss servant mentality and take a deep dive into the art of excellence. We will discuss the importance of *Geri*, which means doing things for the right reason in Japanese. With this type of focus, you will establish a reputation of reverence and respect from many people. You will also cast your net far and wide and attract people who want to follow your work and be associated with you.

Job # 1: A Strong Desire to Serve with Excellence

As we learned in a previous chapter, it all starts with a strong desire. Job number one after a strong desire is learning to set and adhere to high standards, focusing on excellence in everything you do. Job number one is also a relentless commitment to excellence in providing service to others. It is a servant mentality with an obsession for giving your best.

Practicing this attribute makes a statement. With this attribute, you see your work from an artist's perspective. We are speaking about being an artist of life. It's about everything you do is an expression of who you are. Everything matters. It is a statement of pride about who you are and what you stand for.

Kime: The Mark of Excellence

Leaving your mark is a matter of dignity. It is also deeply spiritual. We all have the opportunity to demonstrate our spirit and our excellence in everything we do every day. How we do one thing informs how we do everything. The Japanese term *Kime* means spiritual focus. In this case, the hero's spiritual gift focuses on providing excellent service. It is a focus on giving their very best all the time. Not just good enough, but amazing.

Make your work and every activity a product of who you are. Make your service and actions your sacred signature or "mark." In this way, the hero doesn't give their best for personal accolades or recognition. The hero does it because that is who they are. They understand that excellence is not doing extraordinary things. Excellence is doing the ordinary extraordinarily well.

Heroes don't compare themselves to others. They compare themselves to their absolute best. Unfortunately, too many people settle for terminal mediocrity. They fall prey to the cult of average. Don't get me wrong; excellence is not perfection. Striving for perfection is demoralizing. Conversely, striving for excellence is motivating.

The Spiritual Gift of the Artist

Providing excellent service is giving a little bit more at a high level. Not because you have to but because you want to. It is your spiritual gift as an artist. Amateurs call it talent. Professionals call it practice.

> *"Be a yardstick of quality. Most people aren't used to an environment where excellence is expected."* – Steve Jobs

The Hard Rock Café – Love All, Serve All

My guess is many of you have been to the Hard Rock Café (HRC) at some point in your life. Like me, you may have been lucky enough to visit Hard Rock Cafés in other countries. If not, or if you have never been to an HRC, the chain was started in 1971 by two Americans. Isaac Tigrett and Peter Morton founded the HRC in London. Their idea was to start themed restaurants with a rock and roll twist. They began by covering the walls of their first café with rock and roll memorabilia and offering American fares such as big cheeseburgers and shakes. The twist was that they also served beer, wine, and mixed drinks, not to mention a menu of favorite American entrees.

From its humble beginnings in London, the HRC has grown to venues in 74 countries, including 185 cafés, 25 hotels, 12 casinos, and at least one football stadium that it sponsors. You will find HRC s in almost every major city across the world. They are usually easy to find as they are nearly all in the center city or near significant attractions, as in Orlando.

In April of 2001, I was in the U.K. as a guest instructor of a first-ever Master's clinic in Cardiff, Wales, with a different organization than the one I run today. My family accompanied me on the trip to tour the U.K. after completing teaching duties.

Meeting Ken, "The Keeper of the Keys and Vault"

We had decided to tour London after the Master's clinic. We ended up stopping in at the HRC for lunch somewhere between Buckingham Palace and Hyde Park. Located at Old Park Lane, the original HRC is unique in several ways. It is not only the first location; it is also where many rock legends ate lunch in the early 70s while in London. The Beatles, The Who, and Eric Clapton used to stop by for a burger and a beer.

Eric Clapton was a regular at the original café. He sent the owners one of his guitars and asked to place it over his favorite barstool. Not to be outdone, The Who guitarist and founder Pete Townshend sent a guitar about a week later, stating, "Mine's as good as his! Love, Pete." From there, things just snowballed, and one musician after another began donating pieces of their collection.

After lunch, we decided to visit the HRC gift shop. The original HRC was relatively small compared to others I have seen. What made it even more unique was the gift shop was on the opposite corner of the street in what used to be a bank. The first floor was open to HRC customers looking for their favorite t-shirts and other merchandise, including hats, caps, sweat jerseys, jackets, lapel pins, refrigerator magnets, guitar picks, and about anything else you can brand with a logo. I remember loving the t-shirt and jacket with the words "Love All, Serve All" under the HRC logo.

However, the beautiful electric guitars hanging from the walls like three-dimensional paintings caught my eye the most. At this time, an HRC employee who just happened to be a guitar technician or luthier approached me. I soon found out he was the "keeper of the keys and the vault."

The Spiritual Gift of the Artist

"You like guitars?" Ken said. I looked behind me, and there he stood with his baseball cap turned backward on his head, a goatee, and wearing a leather vest adorned with several or more HRC guitar lapel pins. Ken smiled at me and asked if I liked to play guitar like the ones on the wall. I had barely nodded yes when he asked if I would like to see "the real" guitar collection of the owners. I remember thinking at the time what were the "real" guitars. He must have sensed my confusion as he immediately offered that what hangs on the restaurant and gift shop walls is equivalent to seconds, not the classic original vintage guitars so prized by the owners. Those he said are in the vault downstairs. He then motioned me to follow him downstairs. I asked if my wife, sister-in-law, and mother-in-law could join us. He said, "of course," and off we went past a fancy velvet rope with a sign that stated, "for employees only."

At the bottom of the steps, we found ourselves in a well-lit aisle with several doors and a large bank vault. By large, I mean the type of sizeable walk-in bank vault so standard in banks worldwide. Ken smiled at us and said, "You are in for a treat as we don't show these to many people." He then took a key attached to a wallet chain that you see worn by many bikers. The chain was attached to the belt loop on his black denim jeans. After unlocking a large vault bolt, he used the combination lock with several turns of the dial. He asked us to step back as he opened the massive vault door.

The bank vault had Persian rugs on the floor, and the walls had colorful backdrops. There were also Tibetan prayer flags adorning some of the walls. The guitar vault was well lit, so it was easy to see the treasure within. There were priceless vintage guitars everywhere. One was in an open gun case perched on a green satin stand. It revealed one of Stevie Ray Vaughn's prized Fender Stratocasters. It was easy to see Stevie's famous "S.R.V." on the fretboard. There was also no shortage of guitar stands holding as many as two dozen of the most beautiful electric and acoustic guitars I had ever seen.

I was amazed at the laminated signs indicating who had owned the guitar at one time and, in some cases, what classic rock songs the guitar was played on. I will never forget seeing guitars used by Eric Clapton, George Harrison, Pete Townshend, Jeff Beck, Jimmy Page, Duane Allman, Stevie Ray Vaughn, BB King, Bo Didley, Jimi Hendrix, and Elvis, to name a few. In particular, I had my eyes on a beautiful jet-black Gibson Flying "V" electric guitar used by Jimi Hendrix on the classic rock tune "Red House." Hendrix used this particular guitar during his many early performances from 1967 to 1969. Much later, Lenny Kravitz used the same type of guitar in many of his performances.

Ken said, "you want to play it?" At first, I thought he was kidding, but he quickly picked the guitar off its stand and handed it to me. I remember playing a short "lick" or lead pattern and humbly giving it back to him. He smiled and said, "you see anything else you would like?" I honestly thought I had died and gone to heaven. When I thought it couldn't get any better, I noticed the 1957 Gibson Les Paul gold-top once owned by Duane Allman of the Allman Brothers was only a few feet away. Duane had played this particular guitar on the classic Derek and the Dominos song *Layla*.

Before I could even ask, my new friend lifted the guitar and handed it to me. Again, I played a little ditty and handed the guitar back, hoping not to drop it. I found out later that particular guitar had sold at auction for 1.25 million dollars. Had I known this at the time, I would have probably not had even accepted the offer to play it. Of course, vintage guitars, even those owned by guitar greats, are meant to be played. Just as you would look at a masterpiece such as the Mona Lisa, you must play a vintage guitar to appreciate its value.

The last guitar I asked to look at was a Fender Stratocaster called "Brownie." It also had a laminated sign at the foot of the guitar stand. It was Eric Clapton's main guitar throughout the early Seventies. As it turned out, Duane Allman had played one just like it during many concert performances. Eric Clapton used this particular guitar during his second show at the Concert for Bangladesh. As Ken handed me the guitar, I noticed how worn the fretboard was. The "Tobacco Sunburst" paint finish on the guitar's body was still immaculate, but there was no doubt that Eric "slow hand" Clapton had played many lead solos on this guitar. I strummed a couple of chord progressions and noodled with a lead riff or two before carefully handing the guitar back that was used for the classic George Harrison tune, *While My Guitar Gently Weeps*.

The Lesson – The Spiritual Gift of the Artist

I think about the HRC slogan, "Love All, Serve All," and I think of our experience at the original HRC in London and especially Ken, "the keeper of the keys and vault." I still remember those beautiful vintage guitars. Each one itself is a masterpiece of fine craftsmanship. I then think about the guitar greats or what we can call maestros who played them. These legends pioneered their music genre, style of playing, and in some cases, even the very design of their favorite instruments. Quality is easy to see, and its value is unmistakable. By the way, back in 1986, the collection was valued at $5 million, I was to learn later. What I learned that day was excellence lasts.

I also learned that excellent service is sometimes nothing more than asking the right question at the right time. The simplest things can mean a lot. It can be offering a smile and your passion to others who share the same love. Ken, "the keeper of the keys and vault," showed us through his service how a hero can be not only a guitar god but also a guitar technician who "Loves All, Serves All" through his excellent servitude.

I hope you benefit from this lesson as I did so many years ago. Even more, please take away how the HRC and especially Ken demonstrated the four fundamentals of excellent communication and service. They are:

- **Identify their Identity** – Think about needs, desires, and pride.
- **Relate** – Find common ground and build rapport. Empathize, recognize, acknowledge, and encourage.
- **Share** – Serve others by sharing your passion with as many people as possible.
- **Invite** – Welcome as many people as possible into your sacred keep.

Ken, the HRC keeper of the keys and the vault, did all these things. He identified my needs and desires by asking if I liked guitars. Ken then related to me; he understood my needs and desire. He, too, was a musician and loved guitars. Ken then asked if I wanted to see "the real" guitars. He shared the vault with us. He invited us into his sacred keep.

Quest Challenge: Your Sacred Keep

Take time now to answer the following questions.

1. Do you identify others' needs?
2. Do you relate and or empathize with others?
3. Do you share your passion with others?
4. Do you invite others into your sacred keep?

Your sacred keep can include your home, studio, or wherever you practice your craft or art. You might want to take some time to appreciate it, conduct your Master work in it, and even share it with others who you empathize with.

But most importantly…Do you practice the spiritual gift of the artist? Do you, *Love All, Serve All*?

The Last Samurai

One of my favorite movies is *The Last Samurai* starring Tom Cruise. Captain Nathan Algren (Tom Cruise) is an American military officer hired by the Emperor of Japan to train the country's first army in the art of modern warfare. As the government attempts to get rid of the ancient Samurai warrior class in preparation for more westernized and trade-friendly policies, Algren finds himself taken with the ways of the Samurai, which places him at the center of a struggle between two eras and two worlds.

I love the movie so much because I too am interested in the ways of the Samurai. Perhaps it is my nearly 48 years of martial arts study. I have always been interested in the warrior's way

(*Budo* in Japanese, *Moo Do* in Korean). On the surface, the movie gives the viewer a glimpse into the life of Samura but, on a deeper level, it provides the viewer with a better understanding of **the spiritual gift of the artist.**

Whether it was the way the Samurai crafted their weapons, how they practiced their art, or how they served tea to guests, they demonstrated that everything matters. They exemplified that a man or woman who has attained mastery of an art reveals it in his or her every action. The way they interacted with others on a day-to-day basis was exactly the way they practiced their craft.

As I stated earlier, excellence is not perfection. No one is perfect. But, striving for perfection with a servant mentality is what the spiritual gift of the artist is all about.

> *"The quality of a person's life is in direct proportion to their commitment to excellence, regardless of their chosen field of endeavor."* – Vince Lombardi

As we can see from Ken, the keeper of the keys and vault, every person has the opportunity to share and serve at a high level. As Martin Luther King once said, "Whatever you do, do it well. Do it with excellence. No work is insignificant. All labor that uplifts humanity has dignity and importance and should be taken with painstaking excellence."

You don't have to be excellent all the time. We should, however, strive to be our best when it counts the most.

A Hero Lives the Art

The Spiritual Gift of the Artist

If you are destined to be a janitor or street sweeper, be the most excellent janitor or street sweeper the world has ever known. Do your work like a maestro or a Master. Put one hundred percent of yourself into it. Make your chosen calling your masterpiece.

The key is to try to be excellent at everything all the time, even though you know you will fall from time to time. As long as you get up and try again, you are on the right path. Remember, beating yourself up for failure in life leads to being unhappy and often mediocre or worse at the art of living. It is wise to set a high standard but don't forget you are human. As we <u>ALL</u> have often demonstrated, human beings are already great at being "human." Your job, and mine, is to do our best to transcend it.

Focus on those times that will make the most significant impact on the success or outcome of your moments, hours, days, weeks, months, years, and life. As you focus on doing your absolute best, you are building the excellent muscle or attribute that will lead to even more success down the road.

Use the STAR formula that you now know to identify those few important moments and or projects that need your absolute best. Focus on the high-value tasks first and then move on after giving you the absolute best. Take the time to stop, think, act with excellence, and then review your results. Take responsibility for your product or service. If you don't, no one else will. Remember, it is your mark or signature on it.

Pick the two to three instances each week where delivering excellent service would make the most impact. Start with those first. You will be adding to your list with time as you will be in great demand. Whatever you do, remember, do it with excellence.

The key is to strive for a culture of excellence by setting the example and living by it. The goal is to be a total practitioner of the art, and it starts with a focus on the spiritual gift of the artist.

The receiving process starts with learning, growing, and sharing. Where the rubber hits the road is when we apply our best in service to others. It is the key to success.

There are **eight critical takeaways** to living the art of excellent service. They are:

1. The simplest things can mean a lot
2. Openly admitting mistakes leads to trust
3. In life, you get what you expect and accept
4. The customer isn't always right
5. Quality is always more important than quantity
6. Consistent commitment to outstanding service is essential
7. Assumptions are often dangerous
8. The difference between good and great is often just a little more

212 Mentality

In their excellent book, *212 - The Extra Degree*, Sam Parker and Mac Anderson discuss in detail the concept of the difference between good and great is often just a little more. The critical takeaway is that seemingly small things can make a tremendous difference. For example, at 211 degrees, what is hot, at 212 degrees, it boils. As they aptly point out, with boiling water; comes steam. Steam can power a locomotive.

We can realize the artist's spiritual gift through action, extra effort, commitment, persistence, and additional action. We

The Spiritual Gift of the Artist

attract exponential rewards that are only possible by applying the 212-mentality. It is by giving more that we receive more. By delivering a "wow" experience, we experience a "wow" life.

Decide what a "10" would be and go for "11". Give more than is expected, and you will get more than is expected. You become rich in spirit by giving the spiritual gift of the artist. You receive more than you could have ever realized by providing excellent service to others. Whether speaking, writing, critical meetings, podcasts, videos, seminars, symposiums, classes, or just spending quality time with a loved one, give your absolute best.

Don't fall prey to the cult of average. Require excellence of yourself first. Don't let okay or good enough be good enough anymore. Give that extra little bit that genuinely makes the difference. Whether you are planning to practice or compete, give your best. If Someone asks for ten, give them 12 or 13. Most importantly, please provide them with quality over quantity.

Did you know the average margin of victory in most sporting activities is just a few extra points or a few fewer strokes in the case of golf? In their book, Parker and Anderson mention that the average margin of victory for the last 25 years in all major tournaments combined was less than three strokes. The margin for victory between an Olympic Gold Medal and no medal at all is tiny. For example, in track in field or swimming, the difference between a gold and silver medal is often just a tenth of a second. The same is true in horse races. The exciting thing is that the average payout to the winner in horse races was nearly 400% more than the horse that placed second. Whether you are talking about horse races, car races, or downhill skiing, the margin of victory is typically a tenth of a second or, in some cases, a millisecond.

"When you take care of the details, the score takes care of itself." – Coach Bill Walsh

Prepare for Excellence

Success is a never-ending process; it is the constant pursuit of excellence. There is no end. It is a process of practice, practice, and practice some more. It is a process of refinement, polishing, and re-polishing. It is a process of distilling fundamental basics until they become second nature. It is hard work. It is a **rinse and repeat** process until it becomes automatic. The habit of excellent service is applying the spiritual gift of the artist. Top achievers realize this, which is why repeated and sustained success is so rare. It takes a particular type of mindset that loves giving more than is expected.

RINSE AND REPEAT

The greats have learned that the heroic journey along the Master's Path is a life journey of constant and never-ending improvement. You anchor or ingrain it in the application of excellent service to others. Whether the service is entertainment, sports, business, or religion, the greats constantly give more than is expected. They are remembered well after reaching the summit and moving on to a better place.

To the high achiever, there is no mystery to excellence. It's a never-ending process of refinement. It's a persistent pursuit of better every day. It's not about excuses but rather about doing the work consistently for as long as it takes.

Quest Challenge: Habits of Excellence

Answer the following questions in your journal:

1. Do you prepare for success by planning regularly?
2. Do you give more than you receive regularly?
3. Do you have a weekly plan for living intentionally, and do you use it?
4. How could you improve the quality of your service to others?
5. How can you share more of your unique self with others?

As with previous Quest Challenges, you can set up a scoring system by using two columns to compare your achievements to your desired habits.

As we finish this chapter, it is essential to understand that everything in the universe is either growing or dying. There is no third alternative. In the last chapter, we discussed the X-Factor of Success, a growth mindset. In this chapter, we discovered the spiritual gift of the artist is taking the growth mindset and applying it by providing excellent service to others. We learned that through the giving process, we receive. We also learned that we know, grow, and share most effectively through an exceptional contribution to others. We also learned that we get more than is expected when we give more excellent service.

At a deeper level, we now understand that our spiritual gift as artists is to share and serve at the highest level possible. It requires desire, drive, ambition, curiosity, courage, consistency, and focused energy. Our spiritual focus (*Kime*) is essential to our success. We better understand life and our place in the universe by understanding the Law of Cause and how the spirit of giving is central to happiness and success. As one popular quote states,

"We are all spiritual beings having a human experience."
– Author Unknown

I hope you will continue your journey along the Master's Path with a spiritual focus on providing excellent service. I hope you will share the spiritual gift of the artist. I encourage everyone reading this chapter to explore this subject more fully. Look for ways to use your spiritual gift every day in every way. Make it your sacred mission to give more than is expected and focus on excellence in your every endeavor.

And now, there is not much more to say than "Congratulations!" You have finally made it to the finish line! You have welcomed into your life 16 chapters worth of lessons in leadership and life mastery which have surely been absorbed by your subconscious and conscious mind, and which will serve you well in years to come.

The Spiritual Gift of the Artist

Now, you will most likely put this book away or hopefully lend it to a friend. But your journey has not ended.

Enjoy the first day of the rest of your successful life, Master.

About the Author

John St. James
President and CEO
JSJ Coaching

John St. James has been in the leadership-training business for well over 45 years. He became a certified leadership and martial arts instructor and started his teaching career at the age of 18. John attended the University of California, San Diego. He attained his bachelor's degree in Political Science in 1984 and later an advanced degree in Insurance and Risk Management from the American Institute in 1986.

In addition to being an expert in leadership training, John is considered an expert in personal development through his unique style of teaching leadership skills to those who need it most. John worked for years as a training specialist with State Farm Insurance at their corporate headquarters in Bloomington, Illinois, where he was responsible for producing management-training programs and seminars. John also served on the Board of Directors of the State Farm Federation Credit Union (GA office) for nearly two and half years.

John is also a successful entrepreneur who serves as President and CEO of an international martial arts organization and a non-profit that helps at-risk and disadvantaged children and adults learn the important life skills that are so necessary to happiness and fulfillment. John also serves on the board of two public charities.

A gifted speaker, John enjoys sharing his life's experience with his students, clients, and team members which include doctors, lawyers, educators, and business owners. Mr. St. James is an international certified speaker, coach, and mentor with the John Maxwell Team and is also certified as a leadership coach with the APTSDF, having conducted leadership training in the USA, the UK, Australia, the Caribbean, and Mexico.

> *"Success and achieving the extraordinary is possible for everyone when you choose to…BE THE EXCEPTION."*
> *– Author Unknown*

Made in United States
Orlando, FL
08 March 2024